BASIC ILLUSTRATED
Cross-Country Skiing

J. Scott McGee

Photography by Luca Diana

FALCON GUIDES

GUILFORD, CONNECTICUT
HELENA, MONTANA
AN IMPRINT OF GLOBE PEQUOT PRESS

FALCONGUIDES®

FalconGuides is an imprint of Globe Pequot Press.
Falcon, FalconGuides, and Outfit Your Mind are registered trademarks of Morris Book Publishing, LLC.

Photos by Luca Diana Photography except those by Scott McGee: pp. 1, 2, 5, 7, 11 (top left), 13, 15, 17, 19, 23, 27, 31, 32, 47, 53, 71 (bottom), 78, 79, 80, 81, 82, 83, 104; Craig Panarisi: pp. 30, 66, 71 (top); Jackson Ski Touring Foundation / Andy Canniff: p. 84; and Chariot Carriers: p. 89.
Text design: Karen Williams
Project editor: Julie Marsh
Layout: Sue Murray

Library of Congress Cataloging-in-Publication Data

McGee, J. Scott.
Basic illustrated cross-country skiing / J. Scott McGee ; photography by Luca Diana.
      p. cm.
  Includes index.
  ISBN 978-0-7627-7764-8
1. Cross-country skiing. I. Title.
GV855.3.M42 2012
796.93'2—dc23

                                                        2012022976

Printed in the United States of America

10 9 8 7 6 5 4 3 2 1

Contents

Acknowledgments

To JB and Jan, who hired me for my first cross-country teaching job, and who've remained fast friends over many a season and many miles in between. To Chi Melville, who hired me for my second teaching job and later certified me along with Craig "Pando" Panarisi in telemark at Alta in 1992 and with Jack Bellorado in cross- country at Teton Pines in 1993. To Dickie Hall, my first ski instructor clinic leader in Vermont in 1988. To other mentors, colleagues, and friends: Tony Forrest, Herb Davis, Paul Peterson, Don Portman, Mickey Stone, Deb Willits. Dan Clausen, Urmas Franosch, Jimmy Ludlow, Steve Hindman, Tor Brown, Ross Matlock, Tom Marshall, David Lawrence, Charlie MacArthur, Sam Palmatier, Greg Underwood, Lance Swedish, Leslie Blank, Connie Knab, Bill Goldberg, George Moser, and Paul Smith. To the other professionals in the area who contributed to my growth and development: Scott Wood, Kari Black, Kim Springer, Russ Foster, Steve Neiner, Shirley Kinsey, Dave Field, Rick Simmons, Gene Palmer, Lief Grevle, Scott Nelson, Pat Campbell, Mark Hanson, Dan Miller, Lexey Wauters, Kathleen Roe, and Brian Maguire.

And memorably, to my many firsts: Andy Moskowitz, first return client; John Hubalek, first tele student out west; David Hooke, who put on my first cross-country instructor clinic; Dickie Hall, first tele instructor clinic leader; Mike Keator and Christoph Schork, first PSIA clinic leaders; Mike Stahley, first PSIA alpine clinic leader; Jere Thoreson and Jay Shortsleeve, first PSIA alpine examiners; and Clair Yost, who gave me my first tele powder clinic.

Many thanks to those instrumental in my development as a Nordic instructor of cross-country, telemark, and backcountry skiing: Glenn Vitucci, Carole Lowe, Carson Stanwood, Liz Davy, Russell Rainey, Rich Rinaldi, Rich Reese, David Rolloff, Kurt Gisclair, Tory Hederman, Mark Kessler, Tony Jewell, Deb Payne, Drew Leemon, and Angela Patnode.

Industry colleagues have helped me enlarge the scope of my ideas about cross-country skiing as a sport, as a business, and as an educational endeavor: Jojo Toeppner, John Slober, Jane Dulaney, Linda Crockett, Steve and Judy Over, Mark Dorsey, Andy Hawk, Ben Roberts, Earl Saline, Kyle Hamley, Erin Tulley, Kennon Warner, Karen Hagaman, Steve Over, Linda Crockett, Pete Skavish, Wendy Schrupp, Jessie Halverson, Jim Schnebly, Deborah Marks, Tim Johnson, Steve Lysaker, John Aalberg, Torbjorn Karlsen, JD Downing, Dick Hunt, Drew Barney, Scott Johnston, Midge Cross, Russell Scott, Emily Lovett, Chris Frado, Austin Weiss, Ian Harvey, Jim Sanders, JoJo Toeppner, Rob Lafleur, Eric Rector, Danica Kaufman, Howie Wemyss, Chip Chase, Maurine Bachman, Jessica Workman, Edward Arriola, Bryant Christensen, Lee Bethers, Kerry Clark, Charlie Hazzard, Ellen Guthrie, Art Burrows, Francois Paul-Hus, Julie Meissner, Irwin Butler, and Billy Danford.

I'd also like to thank my suppliers and supporters, without whom I wouldn't be able to keep my skis on nearly enough: Tim Petrick, Jason Newell, Matt Rihm, and Ryan Green of Rossignol, along with Robert Lazzaroni, now with OneWay; Chris Valiente and Collins Pringle of 22 Designs; Gabe Schroder of Smith Optics; Greg Wozer and Melanie MacLean of Leki USA; Tanya Faw and Nate Hanson of Patagonia; Bill Irwin, Steve Kvinlaug, and Justin Morini of Alpina and Crispi; Peter Ashley of Fischer; Ted Wardlaw, Andy Gerlach, Mike Chiasson, Don Powell, and Mike Adams of Salomon; Ian Harvey of Toko; Steve Poulin and Polly Tucker of Swix; Mike Hattrup of K2; Mark Bridges, Mark Warinkios, and Mark Christopherson of Voile; Scott Duer of Asnes; Andy Gerlach of Ski Post; Rick Halling and Sandy Brown of Atomic; Jeff Crabtree and Phil Leeds of Skinny Skis; and my good friend Kevin Hirsh, a talented and caring father and sales rep of many brands.

To my colleagues in the publishing field, Benjam Sadavoy of Ski Trax, Ron Bergin of Cross Country Skier, and Bob and Nancy Gregg of the Master Skier, and to the talented photographers who've helped bring skiing to the printed page, Jonathan Selkowitz, Joe Smith, and Niall Bouzon, and in particular, Luca Diana.

Special thanks go to the reviewers of this text, who have helped me no end to discern clear from muddy and necessary from superfluous: Thomas Turiano, Phil Leeds, Ross Matlock, Eric and Joanne Rolls, Steve Neiner, Chi Melville, David Lawrence, Mickey Stone, Dan Clausen, Doug Elledge, Eric Lipton, Kristen Lummis, and JB Borstellmann, and especially Katie Benoit, Ann Seifert, Laura Case Larson, and Julie Marsh.

No set of acknowledgments would be complete without mentioning my wife, Diane Wardner McGee, and daughters, Lucia and Clara, who have patiently posed for photographs, put up with my long hours at and after work, and been skiing friends and partners on various outings and adventures, from our front yard in Jackson to our "backyard" in the Tetons, and beyond. Here's to many more of the same.

Introduction

When I was 12 years old, a board game called Othello showed up under our Christmas tree. It's the game with an 8-by-8-inch board and chips that are black on one side and white on the other. The game's tagline was, and still is, "Minutes to Learn. A Lifetime to Master."

This friendly learning curve is also true of cross-country skiing in that the simplicity of the sport belies the elusiveness of mastering the simplest of ideas—to balance while gliding on one foot. So, while newcomers to cross country skiing can be "doing it" within—literally—minutes, mastering the one-footed gliding balance of advanced technique can take years. This holy grail of classic cross-country technique may take a few years of practice, though with guidance and training the gifted and athletic may pass this milestone sooner. One skiing truth I live by is this: "No matter how good you are, you can always get better." This is a challenge and a reminder that skiing need never be boring.

Cross-country skiing is a great way to enjoy winter.

As a youth the first book on ski technique that I can recall leafing through was one from my father's shelf—Frank Day's *If You Can Walk, You Can Ski*. It seemed like a sound premise then, and it's still true today, though an apt corollary follows. If you can walk into the Nordic Center or ski school sales office and get formal instruction, you can ski better and farther, have more fun, and work less. Yes, you can ski if you can walk, but skiing *better* is where it's at.

The easy-to-try aspect of classic cross-country skiing provides a big welcome mat for beginning skiers and snowsport participants, and offers continual rewards, even for the expert as higher levels of mastery are reached.

While other activities compete for our time, few can address our cravings for challenge, nature, exercise, and/or social time in quite the same way. However, there are obstacles that keep many Americans from clicking into bindings for a ski outing: travel to the snow, winter clothing, equipment, access to trails, and good grooming. As for money, there are smart ways to keep skiing affordable. Great deals on equipment can be found online and at your local consignment store, especially in snow country. Whatever the hurdles, clear them. You will be well rewarded by many cherished memories.

While, arguably, this book can save you money on lessons, know-how can be another hurdle to clear in optimizing your enjoyment of cross-country skiing. Professional instructors across the country are ready to help you get grounded in your new sport. Skilled guidance in the early (and later) stages can catapult you to new levels of mastery and help you make the most of every ski experience.

Cross-country skiing is family friendly, affordable, and a great option for exercising and keeping in shape. The secret lies in finding or bringing cross-country closer to where you live, or taking the time and making the effort to get yourself and your family to the skiing. Some people have made skiing an integral part of their lives, such that it is literally out their backdoors.

With good information, a little preparation, and some winter manna from heaven, you'll be skiing before you know it.

CHAPTER 1

All That Cross-Country Is

While the name makes it sound like one activity, cross-country skiing actually encompasses a number of ski sports that all have one thing in common: a free heel. In cross-country skiing (often abbreviated to XC), the boots attach to the skis at the toes only. **Alpine** (or downhill) skiers have their heels fixed, or attached, by a heelpiece. While alpine skiers gain greater control for the downhills, higher speeds, and varying snow conditions found at lift-served resort areas, the fixed heel makes getting around on skis more difficult, and walking in heavier plastic alpine boots can feel awkward and clunky. Cross-country gear tends to be lighter and allows more freedom of movement.

Cross-country skiing, also known as **Nordic** skiing (*nord* meaning "northern," as compared with *alpine* from the Alps), relies on skis and boots that are lighter, generally more comfortable, easier to walk in, and arguably much easier to ski in than alpine skis and boots. Indeed, cross-country skiing was born out of necessity—to move around, find food in winter, travel to neighboring towns, or wage war.

One ancient tale of skiing is depicted in a classic painting, *Rescue of Haakon Haakonsson*, that hangs on the wall by my desk: an image of two warriors on skis carrying the infant Norwegian king to safety during Norway's civil war in 1206. The story inspired a famous race in Norway, the Birkebeiner,

Rescue of Haakon Haakonsson by Knud Bergslien, 1869, mysteriously appeared in a garage in Wisconsin and has become an iconic image.

which began in 1932. (It's named for the party that opposed Norway's king in the thirteenth century.) Another classic skiing tale comes from World War II and also takes place in Norway, where special forces hunting and camping on skis were able to sabotage German attempts to refine "heavy water," a key ingredient in atomic weaponry.

All this skiing, out of necessity, often involved traveling great distances. Light, comfortable equipment was key, and the common thread throughout was the free heel.

Today there are (at least) four different disciplines under the umbrella of cross-country skiing: **classic, skate, light touring,** and **telemark/backcountry.** In the coming pages and chapters, we'll take a closer look at the differences in equipment, waxing, and technique for each of these disciplines, and explore the wide world of cross-country.

Classic Cross-Country Skiing

Classic skiing is the oldest and most traditional form of cross-country skiing. Also the simplest, it is the technique that most newcomers to the sport start with. The movements are similar to walking or running, with a prolonged glide at the end of each stride.

Classic is also called diagonal stride; the name "diagonal" comes from the fact that the opposite arm and leg are in front at the same time (as in walking, marching, and running). Classic skiing relies on grip, either via rub-on and smooth-in "grip wax" or by imprinted

Enjoy cross-country skiing with family members of all ages.

"scales" (the first patented "waxless" skis had a pattern resembling fish scales, which was remarkably effective), in the middle section of the ski bases. The walking, jogging, and running movements that this grip allows provide the propulsion behind classic skiing. Usually, a beginner lesson in classic skiing progresses within an hour from walking on skis to gliding and poling.

This is the cross-country skiing that everyone should try. It can take you across a meadow, up an easy mountain, or to the North Pole.

Skate Skiing

Skate skiing, or skating, is a discipline that Americans have claimed as their own invention since the 1982 FIS Nordic World Championships, when Bill Koch used the freestyle skate skiing technique he developed to become the first American to medal at this event.

Skate skiing can be fun and fast.

Skating bears a remarkable resemblance to both ice skating and inline skating. The equipment looks a lot like classic gear, with a few key differences. Skate skis are super lightweight, about 20 to 35 centimeters shorter than classic skis, and have a lower tip profile. Skate boots have a plastic cuff and usually a buckle, and skate poles are very light and quite long—measured from the floor to chin or nose height—to allow longer push-offs at speed and clearance from the skis on uphills. The lightness of the gear (along with the skate technique) lets you really move and cover a lot of ground.

Skating is fast and fun but demands refined balance and endurance to a greater degree than classic.

Alpine skiers, road bikers, and endurance athletes seem to gravitate toward skate skiing for its speed, fun, and fitness value. It can take you 15 kilometers an hour on groomed trails, over a frozen crust, or under rare conditions across a mountain range.

Light Touring

Light touring, an equipment-specific branch of ski touring, is at the core of cross-country skiing. Touring is about exploring untracked snow and leaving the groomed trails and highways behind. For city dwellers light touring could mean exploring with your dog in a city park. "Freedom of the heels" gives you "freedom of the hills." Touring can take you to places near and far and offers a sense of independence, likewise demanding self-reliance. For example, you may need to

Telemark skiing in fresh powder is the ultimate freeheel thrill.

rely solely on your own resources if you are any real distance from a trailhead and are unable to call for help in the event of an incident. Preparedness is key, and traveling with a partner has a number of benefits including having a buddy to rescue you.

Ski tourers must be ready to negotiate hazards, like avalanche terrain, running water, thin ice, downed trees, tree wells, steeper terrain, and cornices, to name just a few. Each tour calls on a different mix of endurance, technique, equipment choice, navigation, and pacing. If you are new to light touring, a guide can be invaluable, showing you where to go and how to get there with the most ease. You will also learn technique and travel tricks, natural history, and ultimately how to safely plan and enjoy excursions on your own.

Telemark and Backcountry Skiing

Telemark and backcountry (tele and BC, respectively) are extensions of cross-country skiing in the sense that a free heel is needed for striding, and both cross-country as well as downhill skills are used. The gear, however, is quite different from the light gear used by classic and skate skiers. The boots are most often plastic with two, three, or four buckles, though some skiers, like another Jackson ski explorer and author Tom Turiano, sometimes still use leather boots (which also may be used for light touring). Tele and BC skis have metal edges for hard snow and durability and are wider for increased stability and flotation in soft snow. Skis for turning also sport more sidecut (wider tips and tails with a narrower waist) for easier turning and carving. "New school" all-mountain skis might also have twin tips (which means a shovel—the upturn at the tip of the ski—on the tails too) and early rise (a long shovel), which make skiing mixed conditions easier and more fun, but which aren't recommended for backcountry.

Telemark skiing (aka tele) takes its name from an area in Norway, where legend has it that Sondre Norheim, father of the telemark turn (and sidecut), jumped over his father's barn, and he later became a Norwegian national skiing champion in 1868. As alpine technique and equipment became popular, telemark slid into obscurity as the alpine (parallel) turn and binding heelpieces became popular in the middle of the twentieth century.

Telemark was often eschewed in alpine skiing literature, but in the 1970s and 1980s cross-country skiers with alpine experience (or vice versa) began taking cross-country skis onto the ski lifts and into the backcountry. Soon skiers were clamoring for better, beefier gear, and many made their own boot modifications to expand the terrain and conditions they could navigate on skis. With credit to former PSIA Nordic Team member Jimmy Ludlow for coining the phrase, tele has become the "SUV of equipment options."

Telemark came into its own as a lift-served sport after the PSIA Nordic Demonstration Team showcased the sport at Interski in Italy in 1983. World Cup telemark racing took off in the 1980s with two events, Giant Slalom with a jump and the Classic Terrain Race, which involves gates, an uphill skate, a jump or two, and a *rappaloosa*, or "noose" loop, in which the racer skis 360 degrees around a tepee of bamboo. Today there is a telemark culture within skiing that spans the range of skiing

Backcountry skiing provides adventure, solitude, and sometimes even untracked powder.

sub-disciplines, including lift-served and backcountry skiing, racing gates, park and pipe, and big mountain "free-riding" and competitions.

Backcountry skiing is the realm of ski mountaineers and powder hounds, snow campers, and passionate explorers. It often involves more difficult skiing, steeper terrain, and the need for knowledge of avalanche hazards. There has even been a confluence of ski mountaineering and the use of lightweight Nordic gear for long tours involving technical ascents or descents.

Backcountry guides are experienced travelers of backcountry terrain who are skilled in educating clients and minimizing risk and who can help you recognize and avoid avalanche terrain. They also can find you the best snow while getting you through the worst snow. From a skilled guide you can learn the skills to travel more safely in backcountry terrain and with more preparedness, whether your goals include free-heeled powder turns or venturing beyond the ungroomed forest service roads. Numerous services are available with qualified guides ready to elevate your hazard awareness and catapult your enjoyment and learning when exploring the wilder side of the winter environment.

The American Mountain Guides Association trains and certifies guides in rock (climbing), alpine (mountaineering), and ski (ski mountaineering). Whether you are looking for a guide or guide certification, the AMGA represents the highest standard of guide education in the United States.

It's beyond the scope of this brief how-to guide to go into depth on the many niche areas of the sport of cross-country skiing, such as Nordic jumping, cross-country orienteering, skijoring (skiing while pulled by dogs or horses), competitive or masters' training programs, sand skiing, roller skiing, biathlon (ski riflery or archery), or even skate ski mountaineering and other offshoots of cross-country skiing. We'll touch on a few of these later in the book, but it's enough to know that there is a wide world of options and opportunities out there in cross-country—enough to keep you engaged, exploring, and fit for life.

Skijoring on groomed trails.

CHAPTER 2 # Equipment

The variety of gear reflects the number of specialties within cross-country skiing. But while each type might have a defined use in mind, most can also be used in a variety of ways. For example, backcountry skis can be used to toodle around the backyard, and skate skis can be used for long tours on spring corn snow.

Evolution

While the earliest cross-country skis were not much more than upcurved planks with leather straps, skis have evolved through laminated wood to foam core and fiberglass to superlight "cap construction" to give racers performance and weight advantages. Downhill ski design has transitioned from skinnier alpine skis to shaped alpine skis, and most recently, nontraditional cambers have turned heads in the alpine, telemark, and snowboard worlds. "Rockered" skis have a reverse camber at rest, and we are seeing more alpine skis with a camber in the middle, not unlike the double camber in cross-country skis. Flex, camber, and stiffness all help determine a ski's response to different conditions and a skier's movements.

Finding the best combination of characteristics for the activity and conditions is the key to having the right tool for the job. A ski that can handle a greater variety of conditions is great to have for a general ski. Embracing skiing is often followed by the rapid development of a "quiver" of skis for more specialized conditions. You might first acquire basic classic skis and later take up skate skiing or want to tour on wider skis for softer snow. While you *can* skate on the wider touring skis and you *can* tour on the skate skis, you'll quickly become aware of how one ski's attributes make it a joy in certain conditions but a frustration in others.

XC Gear Grid

Here is a quick guide to the basic equipment used for the different types of cross-country skiing:

Skate Skiing	Performance Classic Skiing	
Very light; single camber; wax for glide to minimize effort; boots support ankle joint, yet are easy to flex.	Very light; double camber; require wax or klister in the wax pocket for grip, hence importance of flex appropriate to body weight and athleticism. Boots are lower cut, without ankle cuff, and flexible through the ball of the foot.	

Double Camber

Skis for classic cross-country skiing have a different flex pattern known as "double cambered." A double-cambered ski has two distinct bends in it, allowing for both glide and grip depending on the amount of pressure on the skis. The wax pocket is off the snow when it has less than the skier's body weight on it. With the wax pocket off the snow, the skier can glide without the drag of the slower kick wax, and the kick wax is protected from prematurely wearing off by abrasion. Classic skis are waxed with kick wax in the middle and glide wax on the tip and tail.

Recreational Cross-Country Skiing	Light Touring	Telemark/Backcountry
Easy to use; no waxing needed for grip; light and multi-functional; boots not supportive for serious hills, rough conditions, or steeper terrain.	Mid-weight gear; may have full metal edges or metal edges in the middle of the ski; boots are torsionally rigid with 75mm or NNN BC/SNS BC–type soles.	Full metal-edged skis, stiff for hard snow or soft and wide for powder; very beefy boots, most often plastic, with 2–4 buckles and almost zero torsional flex in the sole.

How Double Camber Works

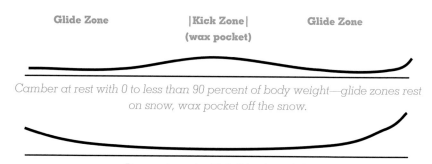

Glide Zone |Kick Zone| Glide Zone
(wax pocket)

Camber at rest with 0 to less than 90 percent of body weight—glide zones rest on snow, wax pocket off the snow.

De-cambered with full body weight
While the curves in the illustration are exaggerated, they demonstrate a key concept that is critical for waxing and ski technique—engagement of the wax pocket and disengagement of the glide zones.

Getting the right skis, with a flex matched to the body weight and athleticism of the skier, is an important starting point. When the skier weights the ski with body weight or greater, the ski will de-camber. The wax pocket will engage and the glide zones will lift off the snow slightly. Because of the way camber works on classic cross-country skis, it is very important to match ski flex to body weight.

Knowing how to engage the wax pocket while negotiating terrain can be invaluable. For example, stepping the wax pocket up onto a snow-covered log or a raised lump or mound of snow on the trail engages the wax, allowing you to more easily cross the obstacle. Conversely, if the grip zone is not touching the snow, but the glide zone parts of the ski are, slipping backward is more likely. Cambers on light touring skis and wider skis for off-groomed skiing will most likely be softer and easier to flex in soft snow; these skis will have a less distinct difference between cambered and de-cambered.

Camber in Skate Skis

Unlike classic skis, skate skis employ a single camber, whereby the skier's body weight on one ski will de-camber the ski to make it flat, with all parts of the base theoretically exerting equal pressure on the snow, for optimal glide. A skier whose skate ski is too soft will de-camber the ski "past flat," which will cause a slightly unstable, plowing sensation as the ski displaces snow, running slower than a ski whose flex matches the skier's body weight.

Ski Bases and Structure

These skate skis have a single camber.

Manufacturers often make what's called a "cold" ski and a "warm" ski, with slightly different flexes for the different types of snow that often go along with certain temperature regimes. They also can provide a base "grind," or structure, appropriate to the temperature range that the ski is designed for. Warm bases tend to come with a warmer, coarser stone grind and are able to absorb extra wax; cold bases are denser to reduce friction and come with a finer grind.

Tracking grooves help the ski go straight.

Boots

While the simplest cross-country boots might resemble lightweight but sturdy shoes, the features of specific ski boots improve fit and responsiveness, affect warmth and durability, and determine the stiffness and weight of the boots. The one main commonality is that the boot sole attaches securely to the binding in such a way as to allow freedom of movement and transmission of power through the boot to affect and direct the ski.

Bar System Versus 75 Millimeter Three-Pin

Modern classic and skate bindings almost all rely on a bar system to secure the boot to the ski.

The 75 millimeter "duckbill" telemark boot became the industry standard. For decades the 75 millimeter sole has been recognized as the "Nordic Norm." In fact the vast majority of all Nordic backcountry boots, including the latest generation of plastic boots, still utilize the 75 millimeter design. (Look for the three-pin holes in the toe of the boot and the three small posts on a 75 millimeter three-pin binding.)

Today the classic leather-hiker three-pin boots have given way to bar system boots for recreational and high-end cross-country skiing, and at the other end of the cross-country spectrum, to stiff four-buckle boots with high cuffs for all-mountain telemark conditions. There are primarily two "families" of bar system soles and respective bindings being manufactured today: Rottefella's NNN system—which includes their NNN BackCountry (BC)—and Salomon's SNS system, their Pilot system being the most current. While similar in appearance, the two systems highlight different features and are not cross-compatible.

Molded Plastic Versus Welted Rubber Sole

Performance-oriented classic and skate ski boots are built utilizing some very sophisticated materials including plastics, nylon, and even graphite carbon fiber. The various boot manufacturers have generally aligned themselves with either Rottefella (NNN) or Salomon for soles, including the binding bar, which is molded into the plastic sole. The latest generation of boots is very light and supportive. Recreational models are generally insulated for skier comfort.

Most tele and touring boots, like hiking boots, have a molded black rubber sole, which is great for walking on snow, rugged terrain, and even around town. Being rubber, however, it bends easily. Thicker rubber and plastic midsole layers increase these boots' torsional rigidity, a key attribute for control in mixed conditions.

Low Cut Versus Cuff

Classic race skis are primarily used in prepared tracks, and like cross-country and marathon runners, cross-country skiers benefit from the lightest possible equipment, using low-cut, cuffless boots.

For skate skiing a cuff with lateral support allows a skate skier's gliding leg to be more "at rest"—a key for efficiency and ultimately endurance.

A medium-weight boot for touring and telemarking improves performance; the higher cuff allows the skier to stabilize the skis in deep or inconsistent snow.

Laces Versus Buckles

Most boots lace in some way, whether the laces are left exposed or covered.

Buckles augment the ease of adjustability and tensioning of the cuff around the lower leg, and one or more are found on both skate boots and medium-weight tele-soled touring boots.

Buckles release at the ratchet. These generally release by pushing the buckle in toward the cuff.

Poles

Poles can cost from $20 for the most basic recreational models to $500 for high-end, carbon graphite superlight and stiff poles for racing. While it's nice to know you can pay just about however much you'd like to, there is a reason that there's a market for high-end poles: The performance (lightness and stiffness) saves so much energy over time that the investment is worth it for serious skiers seeking efficiency and energy savings, whether for speed or endurance.

Let's cover a few specifics you can expect to find on gear for different levels of performance. Recreational poles will have the most basic plastic grips and a simple strap/tensioning system. Performance poles will have some combination of plastic/rubber/cork grips, an adjustable hand-harness pole-strap system, with up to three points of tension adjustability. Being able to customize the fit of the strap to the hand lets the hand relax more rather than always having to guide the pole during the recovery phase. Hand-harness systems often include a quick release feature allowing the strap to disconnect from the grip with the simple push of a button, a great convenience compared to unstrapping Velcro and reinserting your hand after a simple manual manipulation like checking a trailmap or starting a zipper.

Probably most important, and most significant for cost, is the pole shaft material. The least expensive poles have simple tubular aluminum shafts that are heavier and flex under off-axis pressure, essentially wasting energy. Mid-range poles might be simple fiberglass, which are much lighter and stiffer too. Lightest of all are the high-end

Poles with quick-release straps are very handy.

poles that racers use, which are stiff enough that essentially all of the skier's energy input translates to forward motion.

Pole manufacturers often include adjustable poles in their line for three reasons:

1. Touring poles will adjust from about 120 centimeters for downhill to around 145 for classic skiing, with some going higher to accommodate some skating on longer tours.

2. Cross-country poles are made that work for both classic, in the 135–150 centimeter range, and skating, in the 155–175 range. These adjustables are great if you'd like one pair of poles that's good for both, but the adjustability does add a few ounces.

3. Adjustables can be used by people of different heights.

New technologies are emerging for extendable poles, and many of the early shortcomings of the equipment have been addressed. Adjustability will cost—and weigh—more but the versatility is often well worth a few extra dollars and ounces.

Performance skate and classic pole baskets work at a variety of angles as they change orientation throughout the pole push.

Clothing and Accessories

Skiing evokes images of cold, snowy winter conditions, and you might think that bundling up is always the way to go. But skiing *is* exercise, and your body can warm itself pretty well. The best way to dress for Nordic skiing is in multiple layers—generally a base (or wicking) layer followed by an insulating layer and, finally, an outer layer. The more aerobic the activity, the lighter the layers. Common sense and checking the weather will help you dress appropriately. There are, however, some considerations that can help you achieve an optimal skiing temperature sooner and be more comfortable over the long haul. Master these and tune into your body's metabolism and physical needs, and you're well on your way to staying comfortably clothed for skiing and prepared for changing conditions.

Base Layers

The selection of a wicking layer will keep your skin dry and comfortable One of the leading polyesters (i.e., Patagonia's Capilene) or Merino wool works very well to maintain a steady body temperature at different air temperatures and activity levels.

Polyester, wool-blend, and even spandex are great choices for the long underwear base layer for your legs. Wool, fleece, or poly-blend socks for your feet and glove liners of the same material for your hands will help stave off Jack Frost on bitter cold days. Your head deserves a wicking base layer as well to keep in heat that your body could use to keep fingers and toes warm (see more discussion of hats below).

Shell Layers

Two main shell options will help block wind and snow: soft shell and hard shell. A soft shell is a stretchy, snow-repellent fabric laminated to a thin polytetraflouroethylene, or Gore-Tex, membrane. A hard shell is any waterproof layer, whether a laminate or coated nylon. While the soft shell is breathable, it will guard against wind and snow, although in rain it will allow moisture in.

Hats

US Army manuals in the 1970s stated that 40 to 45 percent of body heat is lost through your head. While recent studies put it closer to 10 percent, this is still enough to make a dent in body heat retention. At the same time, strenuous activity can tax the body's circulation system to the point of decreasing blood flow to the extremities. Slowing heat loss from your head means more body heat for your hands and toes. Ultimately we're all susceptible to heat loss through our heads, and a hat can help keep body heat in and make sure the warmth we generate from exercise doesn't go "out the chimney." Personally, I'm a fan of the two hat system, with two very lightweight hats that fit over one another and can be easily added or removed to "adjust your thermostat."

Neck gaiters and buffs are also in this category and serve the same purpose as a scarf—keeping the neck warm. While neck gaiters are thicker and warmer, a "buff" is a Lycra tube. Both are great for protecting chins, ears, cheeks, and noses from sun and wind. Covering exposed skin and closing the gap between neck and jacket are both heat-saving measures as well. The buff or neck gaiter is often combined with a warmer hat.

Gloves and Mittens

Whether protecting your hands from abrasion on refrozen snow or keeping your fingertips warm, hand protection is essential for comfort and ultimately safety when skiing. Gloves and mittens for cross-country skiing come in all shapes and sizes, but there are a few key features that make some work better than others. Gloves provide dexterity and make handling bindings and pole straps easier. Mittens must sometimes be

Lighter gloves provide better grip and feel. Heat from exertion keeps the hands warmer and minimizes sweaty palms that lead to wet gloves and eventually cold hands.

removed for these delicate tasks (another reason to wear liner gloves), resulting in temporarily cold fingers; however, on cold days or during long tours, there's no substitute for mittens for staying warm.

Most XC gloves are fairly light, lean, and spartan, designed to keep an active person's hands warm. Bulkier gloves made for alpine skiing lack the snug fit and dexterity and can soon become too hot for active skiing. Sweaty hands will get cold later, so it's best to find a lighter glove that keeps your hands comfortably warm under most conditions, then add a warmer mitten or more layers elsewhere when it's really cold out. For folks who routinely get cold hands, an extra hat or layers and/ or one of the many types of readily available handwarmers should help. When checking fit, make sure that wrist straps or buckles on the glove or mitten do not interfere with your pole strap.

"Skis, boots, poles; hat, gloves, goggles; skin pro, eye pro, snow pro; food, water, chocolate"—I recite this list like a litany every time I go out. "Skins, beacon, shovel" falls in the middle of the list for backcountry tours into avalanche terrain. This little habit has saved me innumerable trips back to the car, or wishing I'd brought something obvious, like sunglasses, especially when departing on some long tour while it's still dark out. Even on a short tour, it can keep you fed and watered.

CHAPTER 3

Waxing for Cross-Country

Wax is an integral aspect of cross-country ski equipment, especially at the higher levels of competitive skiing. While beginners and intermediate skiers often start with no-wax skis, if they want to wax, they're likely to apply a liquid or paste glide wax when the snow becomes sticky. For long tours or races, serious skiers will go to great lengths to get the best wax job they can. In this chapter we'll cover both glide waxing for skate and classic skiing and kick-waxing for grip in classic skiing.

Waxing with glide wax for the temperature of the day will give you faster skis. Hot waxes need to be melted on, ironed in, cooled, scraped off, and brushed. The wax penetrates the ski base material to make it glide faster. Thorough scraping is key because the waxed base is much faster than any leftover, unscraped wax.

Wax comes in liquid, paste, iron-on, and rub-on forms. Low Fluoro hot waxes address different temperatures and humidity.

Grip or Glide?

Cross-country skiers wax for two reasons: to get better **grip** and to **glide** longer or faster. Nobody likes to slip as they ski up a hill, and while some skiers may not want to go any faster, remember this: It's easier to balance over a frictionless ski and easier to control your speed on a ski that glides well. A well-waxed ski can help you slow down and stop too—paradoxical, but true. We'll look at two kinds of waxing in cross-country skiing: glide wax and grip wax.

Glide

Glide waxes are based on paraffin, the same substance that candles are made of. Chemically speaking, paraffin is simply a long chain of single-bonded carbon atoms with hydrogen atoms, for example, $C_{25}H_{52}$. The longer chains of carbon atoms form harder waxes used for colder conditions. Specialty waxes use additives such as fluorinated wax, graphite, and molybdenum that each address a set of conditions including snow type and age, temperature, and humidity.

To the racer, gliding is "free distance" that you don't have to work for. Slower skis are certainly more work, and in a human-powered sport like cross-country skiing, every little bit helps.

The topic of waxing can be as complex as you want to make it, or as simple as rubbing or wiping wax onto the bases. Wax is applied by one of two methods: using an iron to melt the wax onto the ski, or "crayoning" the wax on before ironing.

For the first method, you melt the wax on the hot iron while moving along the length of the ski. Some like to drip the wax; others prefer to gently slide a corner of the iron back and forth along the base until the wax can be melted into a liquid layer across the base of the ski. Melt the dribbled wax into the ski base from tip to tail, moving slowly and leaving a few inches of molten wax behind the iron. Take care not to burn the wax or let it smoke. If you don't have a digital iron, start with lower temperatures and work up to avoid overheating the bases. Be patient to avoid permanently damaging the bases, and always use the recommended heat or lower for a given wax. Ensure adequate ventilation, especially with fluorinated waxes.

The second method of applying wax is to rub, or "crayon," the wax on and then iron it. Often with "fluoro" waxes, racers and skiers who wax for speed will conserve the wax by crayoning it on.

For hot waxing, a workbench-type area with some ventilation makes a great wax bench. Wax vices work on many tables and benchtops, but waxing can be a messy business, so if you don't have a dedicated space, you'll likely want to employ a tarp on the floor to catch wax drips and shavings.

Structure

Structure describes a micro-level pattern—resembling grooves or cross-hatching—in the base of a ski made by a stone grinder or a rilling tool, which dissipates suction and optimizes the glide surface for snow of different types and temperatures. Structure can be more important than wax in the pursuit of fast skis.

A close look at your bases will tell you whether the pattern is deep and coarse or finer and more shallow.

Look closely at your bases and you can tell a lot about their structure. A coarse grind is good at "breaking the suction" in wet or springlike conditions. Finer grinds work better for cold, sharp, or hard crystals.

Grip

Classic cross-country skiers have two options when it comes to grip. One option entails the use of grip waxes, which resemble harder glide waxes or soft, sticky waxes, which momentarily adhere to the snow to provide classic skis with grip when weighted.

Another option is a **mechanical grip system,** found most often on recreational skis. These "no-wax" skis feature an incut pattern, molded "fish scales," or a unidirectional shingle-like pattern that's part of the ski base. No-wax bases often benefit by the simple application of a liquid or paste wax, especially when glide is compromised in sticky snow.

A waxless pattern is the no-muss, no-fuss way to go. Take your skis to the snow, step into the bindings, and you're off. These bases do warrant some care, however: primarily keeping the bases lubricated with a liquid wax with hydrophobic properties. The lubrication preserves the bases as well as helps the ski glide. Hot waxing is not as effective with the extruded bases common to recreational skis as it is with sintered bases of higher-end skis. This is because the sintering of polyethylene powder

Recreational skis often have some type of mechanical grip system, such as "fish scales" or a shingle-like imprint in the extruded polyethylene bases. Most rental or lower-end skis are made with an extruded base.

leaves pore space between the particles allowing the base to "soak up" more wax. Extruded bases are formed by injecting molten polyethylene into a mold and are less receptive to wax.

The traditional option is to use grip wax. A grip wax for cold conditions, also known as hard wax (though actually softer than the waxes used for glide), is applied to the skis' wax pocket, the middle portion of the ski that the skier pushes into the snow to "set the wax" and stride forward or uphill. For the smoothest, lump-free layer of kick wax, grip the wax very firmly in your hand, and run it lightly over the ski base in the desired zone.

After crayoning on a thin, even layer of wax, use a cork to warm and smooth the wax into a uniform, more durable layer. Not surprisingly this process is known as corking. The smoother the layer, the better the grip and the glide.

How Grip Wax Works

Here's how grip wax works in colder snow conditions: Think of the classic picture of a six-pointed snowflake (known as a *stellar* if two-dimensional or

Corking in some extra blue on a crisp February day. Racers and more serious recreational skiers will use one of a variety of temperature-specific waxes that grip the snow.

The sharper points on snowflakes penetrate the kick wax, giving the skier grip to push off with.

a *spatial dendrite* if three-dimensional). The branches and arms of a snowflake form in the cloud from which it falls, and cold air preserves these as sharp, angular points, which will stick into the grip (or kick) wax when the skier adds pressure during the push-off. Kick wax of the right softness deforms just enough for the snow to penetrate, then the snow crystal breaks away, allowing the ski to glide. Getting the wax right yields a satisfaction beyond description, as a good coat or two of wax will give you all the grip you need on the uphills and all the glide you could ask for on the downhills.

In warmer temperatures the branches of the snowflakes actually start to melt, and eventually the snow crystal goes from being branched to being a much less distinguishable grain of snow. As snow goes through warming cycles, especially melt-freeze cycles (typical in the spring), the crystals lose their original shape and glom together, resulting in larger, rounder crystals with fewer sharp points. For these rounder grains, softer waxes are needed to grip the rounder surfaces. The soft red wax from Swix and Toko resembles bubble gum in its stickiness.

The softest wax for wet or refrozen snow, called **klister,** is a grip wax that comes in a tube and looks like a cross between toothpaste and honey. While many eschew it for the mess it can make, most serious skiers agree that skiing in "klister conditions" can be some of the best, primarily because of the solid grip that klister so often provides.

Applying Klister to Skis

Klister can perform incredibly well in hard-to-wax-for conditions and provide amazing grip and glide. Certain conditions—like a refrozen, warmer, wetter base with cold snow falling; or the opposite, cold snow with wet snow falling—might call for a "covered klister," a klister layer that is then frozen cold and hard enough to spread a layer of hard (kick) wax over the klister layer. The hard wax layer can keep the klister from sticking. This "hard over soft" layering technique is a departure from the typical wisdom for kick-waxing, which is to apply softer layers over harder layers. Variable conditions will give you chances to experiment with different waxing combinations.

As sticky and "icky" as klister can seem, spreading it with your thumb is about the best method, and soon you'll develop your own "clean thumb" technique.

Dab klister onto the ski to get an easily spreadable coat.

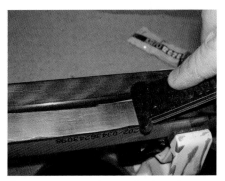

Or use a scraper/spreader to get an even coat. This coat is particularly thick for use in very coarse, wet snow.

So remember, the harder grip waxes are for newer and colder snow; the softer grip waxes are for warmer temperatures with more transformed snow.

When in doubt, one axiom I live by answers the question: "What's the best wax to try first?" The answer is: "The wax on your skis." I often find yesterday's or last week's works fine, and if not, well, it was still the best wax to try first. And if you remember which wax you used and you're close to getting enough grip or not quite getting enough glide, then you can pick the next warmer one (if slipping) or colder (if sticking) and have a better chance of getting it right.

Choosing the Right Wax

To choose the right wax for the temperature and humidity, check the temperature range printed on the tubes of wax. Also check the air temperature and, if you want to get really scientific, the temperature of the snow. You will want to anticipate if the temperature will likely rise, as the day warms up, for example, or might drop, when you change aspect or ski in the shade.

Parking areas often register a higher temperature than just a few hundred feet up the trail, due to the presence of automobiles, dirtier snow, and direct sun. Once you've chosen and tested the wax you think will work, it's a good idea to carry more of the same wax and the next one or two warmer waxes, in the event that your wax starts to slip. If you're slipping, you can apply wax thicker (another layer of the same wax), longer (more toward the tip and tail), and/or warmer (softer and stickier).

Traditional Classic Technique

Classic skiing is more like walking, marching, or running in that the movements are in line with the direction of travel, whereas skate skiing involves pushing to the sides to generate forward momentum.

As mentioned in the introduction, any cross-country skiing can be easy to pick up and learn, but mastery may take years—and that certainly applies the to classic technique. For this reason, starting with sound fundamentals and professional instruction is highly recommended. Before we really get started, it's worth covering a few basic things you'll probably have to do at some point: putting your skis on, turning around, falling down, and getting up.

Classic cross-country skiing can be done with or without groomed tracks.

CHAPTER 4

Getting Started: Classic

Putting on Skis

Most beginner bindings are automatic, meaning you don't have to lift the lever in front (see photo 1) or press the lever closed (see photo 4), instead hearing a "click" when you press down and the binding latches. Here are the steps:

1)

2)

3)

4)

5)

1) *Tap the snow out of the front of the boot and bar by pointing your toe and kicking straight down onto the middle of the binding.* **2)** *Line up your foot with the ski, then line up the bar in the front of the boot over the groove just behind the rubber bumper on the binding.* **3)** *Press the bar into the groove and roll onto the ball of your boot, pressing the front part of the boot into the binding. Automatic bindings will make an audible "click" when the bar snaps into the groove and the latching mechanism is secure.* **4)** *If you are using a manual binding, press the lever that closes the binding, securing your boot.* **5)** *Voilá! You are ready to ski.*

Now, to get comfortable moving around on skis, spend some time with the following basic maneuvers.

Turning Around

Practice these three ways of turning around: 1) On flat ground, step your tips apart with one ski, leaving the tails close or touching. Then step with the other ski back to a parallel stance. Repeat until you've turned all the way around. (Try it in both directions!) 2) Next, try the opposite, stepping your tails apart, moving your skis into an "A" position and then back to a parallel position. Repeat until you've turned a complete circle. 3) Finally, a hybrid of the two approaches lets you turn around more quickly by stepping into an "A" position and then a "V" position. Be careful not to cross your skis.

Falling Down

Falling is somewhat inevitable, so why not understand the safest ways to fall?

It happens to the best of us.

It doesn't hurt as much to fall if you laugh and know how to get back up.

Simply put, fall on the biggest, softest part of your body. In other words, sit down, back on your skis or a little bit sideways. Many a skiing injury has resulted from trying to resist a fall. Sometimes it's better to go for a controlled fall than a failed attempt at recovery.

"What do you do if you fall down?" I ask. "Laugh!" the kids say. If kids (and adults) know this, it takes some of the embarrassment and frustration out of learning to ski.

Getting Up

First, align your skis into a parallel position facing across the hill. Next, slide your downhill ski forward and then walk your hands toward your ski tips. When you can comfortably kneel, you can plant your poles, and then stand up.

Basic Progression

Now let's talk basic progression of skiing. This is the skills/skiing model used by USSA (US Ski and Snowboard Association) and PSIA (Professional Ski Instructors of America).

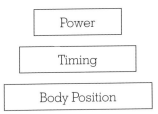

This is a foundational model starting with body position as the basis for building skills. Without proper body position, effort is wasted just in maintaining stance, and power can't be efficiently applied. Once a functional stance is established, you can focus on timing to effectively coordinate movements of different parts of the body. With proper timing, power can then be applied for maximum effectiveness. Without proper timing, effort is misdirected, resulting in inefficient and ineffective technique.

Body Position

Good body position starts with a basic athletic stance, a "ready" position. Because the word *position* implies a static, or unmoving, arrangement of body parts, I prefer to think of this "skill" as *body positioning*, because it's always changing as you ski. An aligned posture, with your hips over or in front of your feet, tends to be most efficient and requires the least muscular support. The "readiness" referred to above is the same you'd expect to see in

Basic athletic stance.

a tennis player anticipating a serve, prepared to move in any direction to return the shot. Basketball players assume a basic athletic stance awaiting a free-throw rebound, so they're ready to move in whatever direction the ball bounces. This basic athletic position is common to many sports and often involves stacking up the body's bones for structural support so most muscles are accessible to use on demand.

Try this: Stand with your feet parallel and hip width apart. Flex your ankles and knees comfortably. Move your hips forward enough to feel your weight shift toward the balls of your feet, and then try to keep your hips forward, tucking your tailbone under, as you stand with weight on both the balls and heels of your feet. Round your back and upper spine into a "C" shape (a healthy "teenage slouch"). Relax and round your shoulders, allowing your head to rest atop your spine with your gaze fixed about 20 feet ahead of you. You should feel forward and in a "ready" position.

Practice balancing in this stance with your eyes closed both indoors at home and on skis, at rest and in motion. Closing your eyes reinforces balancing skills and allows you to focus on optimal alignment and releasing any unnecessary tension being held in any part of your body.

"Falling Forward" Body Position

While "walking on skis" is one way to start sliding and gliding on skis, there is a different approach that many instructors and coaches espouse. This "Falling Forward" technique (not to be confused with falling down) uses gravity to our advantage while creating forward momentum. Whether you've been on skis or not, in order to adopt the most efficient technique, try following these steps before you don your skis:

1. Focus on falling forward. Indoors or on snow, stand in an athletic body position—a ready stance with ankles flexed and hands in front.

2. Start to lean your whole body forward from the ankles, *without* bending at the waist, until you have to step forward in order to catch yourself.

Ready stance (left), falling forward (middle), and stepping at the last minute to catch the "fall" (right)

3. Practice this a number of times until you can consistently fall forward without bending at the waist. You can also practice falling and catching yourself with your hands on a wall or a bar.

4. After falling forward, draw a line with your finger or pole at the back of the footprint that's in front of you, behind the heel.

5. Next, fall forward, placing the *toe* of the boot on the line. Allow yourself to stutter-step, adopting an in-motion falling-forward body position. Strive to step onto a foot that is underneath a forward-moving center of mass.

Drawing a line.

Falling forward to move ahead.

Develop a rhythm with short steps.

6. Next, fall forward again, landing on your other foot. Balance on this foot as you begin a gradual fall again, to the other foot.

7. You are now ready to balance from foot to foot moving forward, still pausing and balancing after each "catch," but with more consistent rhythm.

Falling Forward on Skis

On snow, put one ski on and practice falling forward onto the ski. Balance and glide on the ski. The key concept at this stage is that you can generate momentum with essentially little or no work; falling forward does the work for you. After mastering this on both feet, you are ready for the next step.

With both skis on, balance on one foot and fall forward to land and glide on the other ski. Briefly pause, balancing on the gliding ski, before falling forward again, to land and glide on the other ski.

Link the motion of falling onto each "new" gliding ski into a rhythmic sequence of strides. You are skiing! Practice skiing with no poles and emphasize balancing on one ski. Resist the tendency of the ski you just fell off to "slap" or prematurely land on the snow (balance on only one foot at a time), and always go for a shorter stride over a longer glide.

No-poles skiing. Focus on balancing and gliding on one ski.

Timing

Timing is the second major skill area in the foundational model. Skiing with good timing encompasses **rhythm, intensity, tempo,** and **coordination** of the movements of body parts with one another, as well as knowing when to switch from one technique to another based on changes in terrain, also known as *changing gears*. The result is not only graceful skiing; good timing captures the energy from momentum-producing movements, resulting in increased power and efficiency.

Rhythm

While skiing without poles, focus on moving your arms in a pendulum-like motion generated from the ball and socket joint of the shoulder. The arms swing in the direction of travel. Swing your arms up to shoulder level in the front and as high as flexibility allows in the back. Practice pausing briefly in this extended position, with one arm ahead, and the other back, while gliding on one ski at the end of each stride. You should find that an active, directed arm swing contributes to your forward momentum quite a bit. When you do incorporate poling, this natural arm swing will complement your rhythm and, with ample no-poles practice, be ingrained enough to contribute to forward momentum.

Start Poling

To maintain arm swing timing, add power to the poles gradually:

1. Holding your poles between your thumb and index knuckle, let your arms hang by your sides. Drag your poles and begin striding, swinging your arms naturally as in the no-poles drill above.

2. Continue dragging your poles while adding a slight amount of pushing back, at about 10 percent of your pole-pushing potential.

3. Continue dragging your poles and increase pole push by about 10 percent every 3 minutes or so, focusing on maintaining rhythm and timing the forward arm swing with the forward swing of the opposite leg.

Intensity

The push-off from each foot should be short, sharp, and quick. In this way, de-cambering the ski is optimized and the effort in each cycle is concentrated, allowing more time in between for muscle rest and recovery.

Tempo

Change your tempo and stride length with changes in terrain. Your walking tempo on the flats can quicken to a jog with shorter steps on slight uphills. Easy downhills let you glide out on one ski with a much slower tempo. A great way to increase tempo of the legs is to pick up the tempo of the forward arm swing.

Coordination

In diagonal stride, two main things happen at the same time: 1) the opposite leg and arm swing forward at the same time, and 2) the push-off of the opposite pole and ski coincide. At a more advanced level, skiers

Quick-Quick-Glide

This is a good way to practice balancing on first one leg and then the other to develop a short, powerful kick to lengthen the glide phase. Take two short, quick steps and then glide on the third step for a longer distance. With enough practice you'll develop the balance to stay on the gliding ski longer and longer.

Right ski and left pole are pushing off together; left leg and right arm are swinging forward together. Like a rowing team, coordinating movement of the parts is most efficient and, in the end, faster.

extend the leg they're balanced on during the glide phase, then "pre-flex" the leg as the ski slows down, and then extend the leg again to set the wax and generate power from the push-off. Exquisite timing is what allows the best skiers to ski the fastest.

Changing Gears

In classic skiing the gears are much like those in a car's transmission. Like a vehicle, turnover (rpm or tempo) is higher at lower speeds where more power is needed, and turnover slows on downhills.

Here are the gears:

Herringbone: very low gear for steeper hills; no glide (1st gear)

Uphill diagonal stride: for moderate uphills; may include a small amount of glide (2nd gear)

Diagonal stride: for flatter terrain; moderate glide (3rd gear)

Double pole with a kick (DPK): for slight downhills where double pole works but DPK is faster; the wax is set, the ski stops, and there is a push-off and more pronounced glide (4th gear)

Double pole: using both poles at the same time to increase speed on downhills or flats (5th gear)

Tuck: aerodynamic stance for short or long downhills; neither poling nor kicking would increase speed (overdrive, cruise control, or neutral gear)

Being able to switch gears seamlessly is the mark of a good skier. Graceful transitions from one technique to another optimize speed and efficiency. Rhythm, intensity, tempo, coordination, and changing gears are all aspects of timing that will optimize the application of power.

Power

While body position ensures efficiency and timing places the power at the most effective point in the cycle of movements, applying power becomes second nature only after optimal movements are practiced and ingrained. There are several sources of power in classic skiing: **leg extension** (push-off) and **forward leg swing (kick), arm swing** and **pole push,** and **crunching of the core.** For each, there are two ways to increase power: increase tempo or push harder. Let's take a closer look at each of these.

Leg Extension

Power is applied by pushing down to engage the wax pocket and striding ahead. The wax pocket is the part of the base that is underfoot, and whether it's kick wax or a no-wax pattern that is gripping the snow, it requires compression of the ski in order to push it down into the snow.

Shorter and "sharper" compression achieves better grip. During the short time that the ski has grip, the skier pushes off and gains forward movement. One of the best ways to practice a short "kick phase" is to jog on skis with a fairly upbeat tempo.

Forward Leg Swing (Kick)

At the end of the glide phase the trailing leg should still be off the snow. As the skier moves ahead on the ski that is gripping the snow, the forward swing of the other leg provides momentum that can pull the skier down the track. In order to carry momentum, the forward-swinging leg and ski must contact the snow in front of the other foot. The "slap" of a ski on the snow is a sign of early weight transfer, a common inefficiency in which the leg swing loses almost all its momentum.

Swing and gli-i-i-ide.

Try this: From a standing position, raise one leg back and practice swinging the ski forward, contacting the ground in front of the foot on which you're balanced. Next, try falling forward, as described earlier, while swinging the foot forward. Transfer your weight to the new gliding ski and see how far you glide. Try to glide farther with a more energetic forward leg swing.

Landing and gliding on one ski at the end of a powerful forward leg swing, or kick.

Arm Swing

Like the forward leg swing, the opposite arm swings ahead at the same time, which provides momentum to carry the skier forward down the track.

Try this: Practice skiing without poles. Note how an energetic arm swing contributes to forward momentum. Pretend you're throwing water ahead of you from an imaginary glass held in your hand. This will increase the intensity of the arm swing and direct it in the optimal direction to move you forward down the track.

Pole Push

The poles help propel the skier down the track and have traction on the snow at the same time as the opposite ski.

Try this: Practice skiing with one pole. Focus on the arm swing of the free hand and the pole push of the opposite hand. World Cup skiers use this drill to hone their balance and timing.

A one-pole drill—let your free arm dictate rhythm and tempo to keep your pole arm swinging in time with your strides.

Get the most out of your core muscles to get the most out of your double poling.

Crunching the Core

Whether single or double poling, the core's abdominal muscles are involved in powering the poles. The most efficient application of the abdominal muscles is a quick firing of muscles, resulting in a short, sharp application of power to the poles.

Try this: "Locked and loaded" is a go-to drill for US ski athletes of all levels. Practice double poling with this modification: "Lock" your elbows to your sides and only "sting" the snow with your poles. Do not follow through with your arms or break at the waist. Instead, focus on tightening your abdominal muscles between your belly button and sternum to apply power to the poles. This will train your muscles to fire quickly and powerfully, allowing more recovery time in each poling cycle.

Double poling.

Intermediate Maneuvers

Double Poling

On flats or downhills, it is sometimes beneficial to plant both poles at once and compress the upper body onto the poles. This can be done like the locked-and-loaded drill, using a "short double pole" technique with a high tempo and shorter range of arm swing to maintain speed up a small hill or to accelerate at the top of a hill.

The "long double pole" version uses a slower tempo and full upper body compression, which includes breaking at the waist and falling forward with the upper body until the spine is nearly parallel to the ground. This slower-tempo style can be employed as a more restful technique on long downhills, and it adds speed when gravity is providing forward momentum.

Compressing the upper body in the long double pole, then getting "tall" with hips high and forward.

According to top coaches the long double pole's power comes from getting tall and then actively bringing the upper body's mass "crashing down onto the poles." A longer follow-through results in a lower finish position.

Herringbone

Skiing uphill in a diagonal stride works up to a certain steepness and then the pitch becomes too great and skis slip, demanding an energy-consuming recovery. Instead, use the climbing move that skiers around the world turn to, the herringbone. Named for the track it leaves in the snow, the herringbone uses a divergent stance, the inside edges of the skis, and a rhythmic stride to stave off slipping.

Try this: On a short hill that levels off at the top, stride toward the hill, gradually shortening stride length and increasing tempo as the pitch increases. To transition smoothly from Uphill Diagonal Stride (see chapter 5) to herringbone, maintaining your ski-to-ski rhythm, begin to separate your ski tips into a "V," walking up on the inside edges of your skis. Gradually widen the "V" as the pitch of the hill increases, but be careful not to step on your tails. As you crest the hill, gradually narrow the "V" until your skis are parallel and you are striding again.

The herringbone technique uses the inside edges and a walking or jogging rhythm to enhance grip.

Sidestepping

This is a simple and secure way to ascend or descend short sections of terrain that are too steep to stride up and too deep or uneven to herringbone. Pointing your skis across the hill, stand with pressure on the uphill edges of both skis. Step up or down a few inches with one ski, maintaining the same edge angle and keeping skis parallel, and then step with the other ski to bring both skis together again. Repeat as necessary. Sometimes it is advantageous to sidestep up a slope diagonally, which entails a slightly more natural movement of stepping ahead and uphill at the same time.

Sideslipping

Sliding forward is gliding; sliding sideways is called "slipping" and can be a great way to descend smooth terrain while maintaining a secure position with your skis across the hill. To sideslip, flex both ankles and edge both skis equally. While keeping ankles, knees, and hips in alignment, flatten the skis simultaneously, releasing the edge, allowing the skis to slip downhill while still pointing across the hill. It's important that both edge angles are equal so that your skis start to sideslip at the same time.

Try this: Standing with your skis across a smooth hill, wiggle both skis forward and back (1 to 2 inches) very quickly while releasing the uphill edges to get them sideslipping. This is a way to move past the snow-to-ski friction that can make sideslipping feel unstable.

Half striding, half skating—climbing and traversing—in a backcountry setting.

Advanced Skills for Classic Skiing

While basic maneuvers can take you for miles over hill and dale, there are some additional techniques and technical refinements that can not only be useful, but essential over long distances. Nuances of technique like the "pre-load" discussed below become noticeable hallmarks of good skiing rather than esoterica. Being able to combine subtle efficiencies by upping proficiency in many aspects of technique will allow you to add miles to your tour or shave minutes off your 10K time. Many technique aficionados look to World Cup Nordic skiers to see what the best skiers in the world are doing to be fast and, therefore, presumably efficient with their energy and optimally effective with technique. The assumption that what the fast skiers do is efficient or ideal does not mean that all the movement patterns of the best skiers are simply technique changes within easy reach of skiers who don't train year-round to excel in their sport. For example, it might be more powerful and fast to ski in a lower, more flexed position, but it will certainly tire out your legs faster if you haven't trained for it.

Drills and Skills

Balance Drill

Without skis, balance on one foot and swing the opposite arm forward and opposite leg back; hold the position for a few seconds. Switch legs. You'll learn how to glide longer and get more power out of a coordinated swing.

Swing both arms and the free leg (the one you're not standing on) to develop balance, coordination, and core activation.

Long Glide

On an easy downhill or after a push-off, balance on one ski in the tracks and glide as far as you can. If you can do this in a relaxed stance, it improves balance and opens the door to a longer glide.

Gliding on one ski.

Double Pole Kick

Double poling is great for flats and slight downhills, but there's one technique that can give you more power to get longer glides—the double pole kick, aka DPK. The DPK is a great way to carry some speed up a slight hill by getting added momentum from 1) the forward arm swing with the wax set and push-off, and 2) the forward leg swing accompanying the double pole push.

There are two hallmarks of this technique. The first is a "wax set" where the ski actually *stops*, is compressed, and gets grip for push-off. The second is the forward leg swing—the kick—starting before the pole plant and finishing during the double pole push. So the double pole and the kick happen at the same time. Transfer of weight to the forward-swinging leg should happen after the feet pass.

Try this: Practice the two positions at either end of the DPK technique—extended and compressed. For the extended position,

Double pole with a kick.

Extend!   *Compress!*

stand on one foot with both arms out in front, your center of gravity forward, and both poles about to plant in the snow even with the front foot. The other foot is extending rearward as the hands swing forward in preparation for the double pole. Say "out" as you move into this extended position. The opposite end of the cycle is after the pole plant/ pole push and forward "kick"—the finish of the leg swing. Say "in" as you move into this compressed position. You can use your own mantra to maintain a rhythm and coordinate upper and lower body positions.

Leg Swing Drill: Airplane Landing

Try this: Standing on one ski, lift the other behind you and prepare to swing it forward. Flex your rear leg's ankle and knee *slightly* to allow a smooth landing in front of your other foot. (With enough of a high, forward hip position you can easily add power to the leg swing and land it in front of the foot you're standing on.) Swing your leg forward and bring it to a stop with your feet even. If you've captured the energy of your leg swing, you will glide forward few inches. This is the free distance you get with every double pole kick cycle.

Now do the same drill *the less effective way:* Try the leg swing with a longer, stiffer leg and/or your hips slightly low and back. You'll find that your ski slaps the snow every time. If your foot were the airplane,

Leg swing drill with airplane landing (left). Flex ankle and knee (middle). Smooth landing (right).

this would be the landing in which the pilot forgot to pull up on the controls and landed at too steep an angle—and short of the runway. You'll also find that the leg swing's forward momentum is lost in the impact of the ski on the snow, and you won't glide forward at all.

Lower Leg Compression, Flexion, or Pre-Load

Pre-load is not a universally agreed upon term, but it's a good way to describe a hard-to-observe phenomenon, the pre-flexing of the glide leg prior to the wax set. Flexion in this leg effectively increases the range of motion and the degree to which the skier can push off.

Uphill Diagonal Stride

Uphill skiing doesn't so much require its own different technique, but simply some modifications to diagonal stride: shorter stride lengths, higher tempo and impulse, a definitive wax set, and a continuing focus on an effective body position that allows it all to work. Impulse is a term from physics where $i = f/t$, or impulse equals force divided by time. A hammer resting on a nail for an hour won't drive it, but a swing—hammer in contact with nail head for a fraction of a second—will put it into the wood.

Likewise, a skier can achieve grip on hills with a short, sharp increase in pressure to the ski, most simply described visually as jogging up the hill. This high-impulse pressuring of the ski de-cambers the ski, pressing the wax or scales into the snow for better grip. Once mastered, skier can direct energy less toward the up and down movements associated with jogging and more toward the direction of travel.

Freestyle Skate Ski Technique

Learning to skate ski requires a higher level of skill than classic because it relies on one-ski balance, but relative mastery comes earlier. Once skiers learn balancing and gliding on one ski, pushing off an edged ski, and basic pole timing, they can handle most terrain. Skate skiing gets easier with speed, much like riding a bike.

Skate skiing can bring the ultimate reward, "crust cruising" over the surface of smooth refrozen snow, often in the spring on cold, clear mornings.

CHAPTER 6

Getting Started: Skate Skiing

Body Position

An efficient stance is key for skate skiers. To achieve the best body position for skating, adopt an athletic stance, with knees over toes, hips and shoulders over feet, and a rounded back. Many coaches refer to this as being "stacked," which is one way of saying that your body parts are in alignment and minimal muscular effort is needed to maintain balance.

Stand with your ankles flexed. Looking down, extend and flex your ankles to move your knees back and forth to cover your toes. A skier who is "back" (below right)

Stacked.

Back.

Practice a forward body position by tipping your whole body forward (left) and catching yourself (right) by stepping into a "V" and balancing. Shorten the step and keep falling and stepping to stay in a forward position.

can't access the full range of motion needed for an optimal push-off.

Start with the basic athletic stance described for classic skiing, only allow your feet to form a "V" such that your (imaginary) ski tails would not cross. Press forward from the ankles tipping your whole body forward. This is much like the practice of falling forward described for classic skiing in chapter 4.

Rockin'

Facing up a slight hill, with your feet or your skis in a "V," practice a rhythmic stepping from one ski to the other. Balance momentarily before moving back to the other ski. The ideal motion of the body is side to side, as if your hips were sliding directly sideways along a smooth

Rock in a "V" to develop your balance, rhythm, and forward body position.

rail from left to right and back, without tipping your body at the waist, twisting in the hips, extending into a taller stance, or flexing into a shorter stance.

V-Flex Drill

To get the skis moving, skiers must first understand that generating momentum can come simply from an effective body position, and that adding power (from leg extension/push-off) should come later. In a level area, assume an athletic stance with your feet apart and the skis in "V" shape, tips pointed out at a 30- to 40-degree angle, which should put the skis slightly on edge. Stand with your hips over your feet in a relaxed, healthy "teenage slouch."

To experience body position–initiated movement, press forward at *the ankle joint*, taking care not to bend at the waist (page 57, left). The flex in your ankles will push outward on the skis, and you will begin to slide forward (middle). Pick up one of your diverging skis and step it

V-flex drill.

back underneath you to prevent doing the splits, like Bambi on ice, then glide to a stop to repeat this drill (right).

The preceding exercises all underscore the importance of body position, and how propulsion can be generated simply by adopting an efficient body position. To summarize simply: The skier stands with his/her center of gravity in front of the feet. This creates the sensation that the body is falling forward from the ankles. In reality, the skier maintains forward body lean and extends a foot and ski to catch the "fall" and capture the momentum of the body's forward motion while balancing on a gliding ski. With good body position, skiers are ready to develop timing and then add power with leg extension and core body movements.

Timing

When skaters think of timing, they often focus on pole timing in relation to ski landing or leg push-off and the different gears that these different timings represent. But timing also pertains to weight transfer and edging the skis, coordinating movements of the arms and legs, and changing gears to anticipate changes in terrain.

Weight transfer refers to the moment body weight leaves one foot and moves onto the other ski. Many skate skiers are reluctant to get "over" their new glide ski. Rather than commit to the new ski and achieve an effective resting stance, even if only momentarily, they fall back to the other ski. Skiers will get the most out of the weight transfer itself if they flex their ankles in time to push off an edged ski in the optimum position. This aspect of timing is quite crucial to effective and efficient skate skiing.

Power/Propulsion

Power in skate skiing comes from the push-off of the leg extension, from "leg drive" of flexing forward in the ankle joint during the glide phase, and from poling and the forward arm swing (recovery). Push-off power is more gradual than in classic skiing, and happens through the glide phase, with a snappy finish. This push-off propels a skier forward and onto the opposite ski. Accuracy in the direction of the push-off and the power of the push-off determine the length of the glide on the "new" ski.

The power from the pole push is almost exactly like the short double pole in classic skiing, except that it must be wider due to the wider stance in skate skiing. The pole push and arm swing will be more closely aligned with the direction of travel in higher tempo (slower speed) skating and more in line with the next ski in slower tempo (higher speed) skiing.

Skate skiing, like classic, relies on the fundamentals of body position, timing, and power. Refine each of these elements to ski efficiently (least work) and effectively (best result). In the next chapter, we explore some of the different pole timings to adapt technique to different terrain.

CHAPTER 7

Advanced Skills for Skate Skiing

The "gears" in skate skiing refer to different timing of leg flexion and extension with pole push and arm swing/ recovery. Knowing each gear and when to use it is one thing; switching seamlessly between gears is like having a smooth transmission in your car and allows the skier to carry more speed through gear changes.

The Gearbox

Skate skiing has five gears—Diagonal V-Skate, V1, V2, V2 Alternate, and V0 or No Pole Skate. Each gear is suited for different terrain and different speeds and is distinguished by its own timing of the pole push and arm swing in relation to the compression and push-off of the legs.

Diagonal V-Skate

Also called gliding herringbone, diagonal V-skate is the lowest gear, great for steep hills and going slowly to avoid overexertion. Some big old pickup trucks have a L1 or "low first" gear, and the diagonal V-skate is the low first gear of skating. Skate skiing seems to require a "critical speed" in most of the other gears, in part because all the other gears have at least some phase where the skier must balance on one ski.

One ski and the opposite pole push off at the same time in the diagonal V-skate.

In the diagonal V-skate, one ski and one pole are always on the ground, steadying the skier and allowing for more relaxation of the non-firing muscles. Start by walking in a "V." The marching-like step (encouraging diagonal movements) will establish the opposite leg/arm movement coordination. Add glide to each step to begin skating. Try pushing with the opposite arm and pole as you step up/swing forward the opposite ski and pole. Although you'll rarely see this maneuver in a race because it's also the slowest gear, it is a good one to have in your repertoire to climb hills at a sustainable pace. Gliding herringbone can be an easy way to learn and practice skating.

V1 Skate

The V1 skate is the gear for uphills, with both poles and one ski providing propulsion at the same time. V1 is also used to get started from a stop, just like first gear, or any time the going is slower, like very cold snow or skating through a layer of fresh snow. The V1 is one of the easiest techniques to grasp, and some say it's the best to learn first, especially if the terrain available is rolling in nature. Due to the asymmetry of the V1, the ski-side hand, called the "hang pole," is held higher with a steeper pole angle. The push pole (or the offside hand) is held lower (around your chest) with less angle. A good general guideline is to plant the poles near your feet, maintaining functional tension in your core, ready to push.

Three-One

Two poles and one foot make up three points of contact. The arms recover while the skier is balanced on the other ski, with one point of contact.

Try this: Balance on one foot with poles in hand, but both skis off. Rock onto the other foot, making both poles come down at the exact same time as the foot. Next, try it with skis on.

Stand on one ski and place both pole baskets by the corresponding feet. This is the "3" position, because there are three points of contact. Rock sideways into balance over the other ski with poles off the snow. This is the "1" position. Establish a rhythm, rocking from the 3 position to the 1 position and back, always coming into balance in a flexed-ankle stance. Take care that all three points of contact hit the snow at exactly the same time.

The V1 gets its power from the combined force of the upper and lower body at the same time, just as rowers on a crew team pull on their oars at precisely the same time. Just use the poles lightly at first, be careful to not lose the good body position we've been working on. A

The right ski and poles contact the ground at the same time (3 points).

After the completion of the pole push, the left ski will become the one point of contact.

common mistake at this point is to use the poles too much and forget about using the legs.

Having established a rhythm and synchronizing the three points of contact, you're ready to glide ahead. Do so with short glides in which you keep moving forward as described previously.

V2 Skate

The V2 is a good "second gear" for flatter terrain or for carrying momentum up the beginning of a hill. Sprinters will use V2 or a variation of it for all but the steepest terrain. In my own skiing experience, it was a breakthrough when I found I could not only use the V2 on the flats, but when going uphill as well.

It is easy, particularly in the early learning stages, to ski the V2 inefficiently. Two keys to greater efficiency are 1) to master gliding in balance over one ski, and 2) to correctly time upper body compression and lower body extension. While balance in the V2 skate is critical for efficiency, it is the gear that alpine skiers often learn "accidentally," making its timing a transferable skill for new skaters who are not new to skiing.

Hop-Skate Recovery

Try this: Stand in balance on one ski and begin to tip over too far across the ski—falling to the *outside*. Hop your ski to the left to create

If you start to tip too far left onto the outside edge (left), hop the left ski out and to the left onto the inside edge (right), and you won't fall over to the outside.

a bigger "V" and move the ski to the outside, allowing the body to "fall" between the skis. This drill establishes better balance and allows skiers to glide over the ski—which is critical for learning the V2.

The key timing skill is staying over one ski and completing the upper body compression while in balance over the flat ski. A cagey Nord knows "that a flat ski is a fast ski." So optimizing glide time contributes to overall efficiency. And falling in the direction of the "new" ski too soon edges the ski you're currently balanced on, slowing you down. The V2's quick forward arm swing and near-vertical (double) pole plant and compression, all need to happen while balanced over the gliding ski, and before the push-off to the next ski.

V2 calls for a complete pole push (compression) before pushing off with the skating leg. Use the cue: "Pole, skate . . . pole, skate" where "pole" is the compression (down onto the poles) and "skate" is the push off the edged ski onto the new ski accompanied by the forward arm swing. Another useful mantra is "Glide, pole-skate, glide, pole-skate." It's important to remember to glide, balanced on the new ski, before the poles come down or else you're just V1-ing on both sides—one of the most common V2 "errors." Remember to complete the pole push before pushing off with the skating leg. The compression of the upper body is accompanied by compression of the legs as the ankles and knees flex, giving the legs plenty of range to extend, creating a strong push-off.

(Left to right) Ankle flex and pole push (compression), push-off and pole follow-through, glide phase with arm recovery, and pole plant in anticipation of the next compression make up the cycle of movements in the V2.

V2 is great for slight downhills, flats, and even short or shallow uphills and uses a pole push to elongate the glide.

V2 Alternate

The V2 alternate is the gear for flats and slight downhills. Poling occurs on one side only, between skates.

Try this: Leave your poles on the side of the trail and practice skate skiing like a speed skater, with one hand behind your back. This will develop the feeling of generating momentum with a powerful forward arm swing during the push-off on the opposite ski's edge.

Next, swing *both* arms forward with the same timing used for the speed skater drill. Finally, get your poles and integrate a double pole push into the skating. Both poles swing forward during the push-off of one ski, and then a complete double pole plant and push will bring you back onto the other ski.

Skating in a tuck.

V0

V0, the "free skate," is simply skating with no pole plants; it's used when speed exceeds pole push effectiveness.

CHAPTER 8

Downhill Techniques

The skier's responsibility code says, "Ski in control at all times." Ultimately this means one thing: You must be able to stop—even if that means sitting down.

Most cross-country trails are a blend of easy, rolling, and hilly terrain, but certain areas should be attempted by skilled skiers only. Know what kind of terrain you're heading for. Bringing a map, a friend or a guide, and the right equipment can make or break an outing.

It's useful to learn a few downhill skiing concepts. First let's consider the *fall line*, often described as the direction water would flow or a ball would roll down a hill, i.e., straight down. To manage speed with turns, you must ski through the fall line, which is a committing sensation and one best approached with confidence and the skills to keep you on your feet.

Alpine skiers break skiing down into four types of movements: **balancing, edging, rotary,** and **pressuring.** The emphasis on movements is important because while body part movements often tell a story, being able to focus on specific muscle movements is more useful to the apprentice of the sport.

Balancing movements include staying over your feet, visually anticipating the effect terrain and snow have on balance, and balancing on a flat ski (because a flat ski is a fast ski).

Edging movements originate in any of the "side-bending" joints, including the spine and hips, knees, ankles, and the bones and muscles in the feet. It is in fact these finer movements in the feet that are critical for braking and turning, which both involve skidding, in which the skis slide both forward and sideways over the snow.

Rotary movements involve turning the skis, most often by turning the ball-and-socket joints of the hip, knee, and ankle. Rotary movements are used to skid the skis into the wedge stance for braking or into a parallel or tele turn, and even to keep the skis pointed straight.

Pressuring movements include both flexing and extending, most noticeably in the joints of the ankles, knees, and hips. Jumping and landing involve pressuring movements.

Work your way through these milestones of skiing to build the skill base you will need to help you ski in control at all times.

Slowing Down and Stopping
Wedge

To slow down or stop using a wedge (also known as a snowplow), step or smear your skis into a "V." Flex your ankles enough to bring your knees over your toes and roll onto your inside edges equally. The wider the "V" or the higher the edge angle, the faster you'll slow down or stop.

Half Wedge

The half wedge can be a more secure way to descend hills. Leave one ski in the track and use the other ski, edged and in a "V," to do the work of the wedge. Flex both ankles and make a "V" with your skis, keeping the tips even but not touching. Increase braking power by using more edge and widening the wedge using the ski outside the track.

Turning
Wedge Turn

To make wedge turns, establish a gliding wedge in which the skis are on equal edge angles and the "V" remains the same size. By lightening the pressure on the inside edge of one of your skis, and turning both feet, you can turn in that same direction. For example, lighten the right ski and turn both feet (legs) to turn right.

Wedge Christie

The wedge christie is a step between the wedge and a parallel turn. Finish a wedge turn and, at the end of the turn, change edges to roll both skis onto their uphill edge, steering the skis together through the turn's finish.

Half wedge turn.

Parallel

To make parallel turns, tip both skis downhill at the same time. Apply a steady but firm steering (turning) motion with both feet to guide the skis into and past the fall line while the skis are flattened and easy to turn.

Telemark

The telemark stance involves a fore-aft separation of the feet, leaving your weight on the whole of the front foot, but solely on the ball of the back foot. As with a parallel turn, tip both skis together and steer both skis into the turn.

Stepping, turning the ski, and pushing off to skate through a corner.

Cornering

Sometimes the best way to change directions is to step the skis around a turn, one ski at a time. Step turning is a series of quick, short direction changes for downhill corners. Cornering in this fashion requires stepping from one edged ski to the next and can be enhanced with a push-off, making it a skate turn. The active push-off allows the skier to generate power and gain speed through a corner.

Kick Turn Traverse

A useful skill for descending without having to point your skis down the hill, this is a version of the uphill kick turn, but with the goal of descending via a series of switchbacks with downhill traverses. To begin, point your skis slightly down the hill and traverse, gradually losing elevation, until terrain or trees dictate a stop. Skid or step the skis perpendicular to the fall line. Do a kick turn by lifting your downhill ski and placing the tail of the ski where the tip just was, adjacent to the tip of the other ski. Pivot on the ski and, by opening your hip joints, transfer all your weight onto the downhill ski. Step the other ski around parallel to the first ski, and you're ready to traverse across the hill in the new direction.

The Tuck

Most downhill techniques involve turning to check speed or manage the rate of descent. On downhills in a race, or for the pure thrill of it, skiers will try to get the most speed that gravity will give them, minimizing drag from the air and going straight down the hill in an aerodynamic tuck position.

Assume an aerodynamic position on the downhills to minimize wind resistance and maximize speed.

CHAPTER 9

Training and Safety

Training

Many skiers approach ski fitness with the idea that they can ski themselves into shape. Real benefit, however, can be realized by following a general or specific pre-season training plan, known by many skiers as "dryland training," and then following a formal or informal program of actual ski training throughout the winter. There are immense benefits to entering the ski season with weeks, months, or in the case of elite athletes, years of physical training. Likewise, in-season training will produce optimum results when you focus attention not only on how to ski (technique), but also on

Roller skiing is a great way to maintain balancing skills and muscle-specific fitness in off-season dryland training.

when to apply different types of training and when to rest. Some basic tenets of training follow.

General Training

"Building a base" is about general aerobic fitness, training for longer durations, and long distance with low intensity. This might include "cross training" or workouts in another sport (including classic for skaters, or vice versa), to improve overall fitness or to strengthen a different set of muscles or different muscle groups. Skiers who cross train—be it running, biking, field sports, paddling or rowing, or other endurance or core-fitness activities—typically achieve higher fitness and better results because of it.

Specific Training

Often focused on a specific aspect of technique such as bounding up a hill or double poling, specific training also includes concentrated bursts of power for short durations to build strength and explosiveness.

Training Levels

Based on your tested or estimated maximum heart rate (MHR), training levels denoted as 1 through 5 describe a certain percentage of your MHR. Plan your level of workout using percentage of MHR to achieve specific goals such as endurance (base), strength, and speed.

Level	Percentage of MHR	Description
1	60–70	Distance; easy, conversational pace
2	70–80	Distance and technique
3	80–90	Threshold training
4	90–95	VO_2 max training
5	95–100	Speed and overspeed

Periodization

Planning cycles of building, peaking, and recovery in your training—by the day, week, month, and year—requires athletes and coaches to appropriately schedule base building, intensity, and rest to optimize performance and readiness for competition.

Great resources for training in general and cross-country ski training in particular can be found online and in your local bookstore.

Safety
Trail Code

There are risks in skiing that common sense and personal awareness can help reduce. It is important to be safety conscious. This is the cross-country skiers' responsibility code:

- Ski in control at all times and use extreme caution when skiing downhill.

- Ski in a manner that does not endanger others.

- Never stop where you obstruct a trail or are not visible by others.

- Obey all signs and posted warnings. Keep off closed trails.

- People ahead of you have the right of way. It is your responsibility to avoid them.

- Be prepared and know your limits.

Etiquette

Beyond the skiers' responsibility code, there is a set of customs that lie somewhere between safety and courtesy. For example, in the days before grooming, if a skier fell down and messed up the tracks, the polite thing to do was to fill in the "sitzmark" and repair the track. While this rule now seems somewhat antiquated, it is worth noting the intent behind it and our shared responsibility to keep the trails in good shape, especially where ungroomed. Another example of etiquette is to always yield to a skier skiing downhill toward you.

Routefinding

Staying "found" and safe involves a set of skills including navigation, avalanche awareness and avoidance, and emergency preparedness.

Whether it's a map and compass or GPS, know how to use these tools and how to read a map, choose a route, and pinpoint your location.

Navigation can be as simple as following a road out and back or as complex as using a map and compass to navigate thick woods or rolling hills in a foggy whiteout. Global Positioning System (GPS) technology has revolutionized the access to real-time mapping capabilities that under some circumstances can render the paper map and magnetic compass antiquated. Technology does have limitations, however. Open sky is needed for GPS to position the user on the map, and many units require the loading of all relevant maps. Many outdoor recreationists are using iPhone or Android apps to chart routes and track progress, but these mapping apps often require a broadband connection for topographical data, and here too the technology is reliant on adequate signal strength to be effective.

Routefinding is a hard-won skill because learning to read terrain is a skill born of experience and mastered through mistakes. Most people take years to develop the combination of intuition and experience that makes a good routefinder. Staying on established trails might seem safer, but masterful routefinding can sometimes actually be safer, and besides, exploring is a big part of adventure.

Frequently, snow cover in woods or meadows makes following a trail more difficult than reading terrain and making a trail of your own. With practice you can improve your route by striking out on a bearing and finding a straighter path through the woods, or by reading the terrain ahead to find the path of least resistance. Being the first to break a trail comes with a special responsibility to all who follow, since it is almost always easier to follow already-laid tracks than to break a new trail.

Using map reading and routefinding together to avoid potentially hazardous terrain, you can negotiate your route with confidence, knowing where you are at all times. Part of the art of tracking your location on the map involves keeping it handy and referencing not only man-made trails and roads, but also natural landmarks like ridges, ponds, streams, ravines, and meadows. Often a sweeping view of the route ahead can provide a good opportunity for "dead reckoning," the practice of sighting a landmark and then progressing toward it through terrain changes, via compass, orienting by the sun or referencing off distant landmarks like a peak at the head of the valley or the walls of the canyon or drainage you're following. Practice and mileage will eventually impart experience, of both dead ends and secret passages, that will help you find your way when the way is not clear.

Some routefinding techniques include:

1. Following contours to maintain elevation when picking a route is easy.

2. Avoiding steep terrain where small obstacles can become large ones, such as when, for example, you have to maneuver up or down around an impassable log.

3. Staying away from creek beds and canyon bottoms, which often meander or have steep-walled bends, making for difficult terrain negotiation.

4. Scanning and connecting with the terrain ahead in the most efficient way possible.

5. Setting a low-angle track or switchbacks if necessary and appropriate. Steep tracks demand a lot of energy to put in and to follow.

6. Minimizing avalanche hazard by avoiding being on or below slopes 28 degrees or greater in steepness. Phone apps are available that use geographic (GIS) information and are fairly accurate.

When following tracks, consider: Were these tracks left by novices or experts? Do they follow the best route? Do they avoid avalanche hazard? Are there corners worth cutting, or foreseeable obstacles or hazards worth circumnavigating?

Practice reading maps and routefinding with your partners. In the event of an incident, it may be critical for them to be able to navigate back to civilization and describe your location over the phone. Keeping your group clued in to the map and the general plan also helps with another key aspect of group travel.

Staying "found" also means staying together as a group. Many searches have stemmed from a party allowing itself to become separated. It's often helpful to have one person act as a routefinder/trailbreaker in front, with the slower skiers close behind and a strong skier as the caboose. Staying within sight and sound is a good guideline. Tune your entire group into the navigation plan so that everyone has a general idea of where you're going. Ask everyone to regroup at intersections, or if a trail is clearly marked, you might choose a few key points along the route to meet.

Winter Hazards

To stay safe in a winter environment, you must be aware of the signs and treatment of cold-weather hazards, such as frostbite and hypothermia, as well as be prepared for incidents that might involve first aid or equipment repair.

Frostbite occurs when skin gets cold enough to freeze, inflicting permanent damage when blood vessels burst in the thawing process. If you get very cold hands or feet (numbness) or see any white areas on another person's nose or cheeks, take immediate action. Return to a warm environment as soon as possible. Warm up cold extremities in warm water (95° F) *only* if you're positive you can keep the body part warm. If fingers or toes are truly frostbitten, thawing them only to have them refreeze again can not only be very painful, but also can do more damage than simply letting them stay cold until you're back in a controlled environment. For cheeks and noses that exhibit signs of frostbite (whiteness), a warm hand on the face to help rewarm the surface of the skin is the prescribed treatment. Rubbing can do serious damage and should be avoided.

Hypothermia occurs when the core body temperature drops below 95° F. Symptoms include disorientation, confusion, loss of coordination, irritability, and the "umbles," so called because the victim will mumble, fumble, bumble, stumble, and grumble.

Someone who is hypothermic may not be able to self-rewarm through exercise or even by going inside. Treatment includes removing wet clothing and replacing it with dry layers. Ingesting hot liquids and crawling into a warm sleeping bag with hot water bottles are also ways to aggressively treat hypothermia. Hypothermia victims whose heart rate has slowed a great deal may appear to not have a pulse but might still be alive. It is important not to disturb patients in this state because of the possibility of cardiac arrest. Once rewarmed, a victim of hypothermia may be tired or even exhausted, but with hydration and rest can usually fully recover in a short period of time.

First Aid

Readiness for accidents—major and minor—begins with a knowledge of first aid and having the proper equipment to respond in situations requiring first aid. Training in first aid is available through the American Red Cross, the Wilderness Medical Institute, and numerous other providers. Courses that focus on wilderness first aid include protocols for emergencies that occur more than 2 hours from professional care and are highly recommended for anyone planning to spend time where medical help is more than a phone call away. Ski patrollers take a version of first-aid training called Outdoor Emergency Care, and many guides and expeditioners complete a course such as Wilderness First Responder (fewer than 80 hours) or Wilderness Emergency Medical Technician (fewer than 160 hours).

Next, having the right first-aid kit is essential. If you have a kit like a mobile operating room with everything from bottled oxygen to sutures, it will be bulky and weigh so much that you might choose not to take it with you. If your kit is *too* small, however, you may not have the things you need or enough supplies for a major incident.

A basic kit will include:

❑ Band-aids

❑ Moleskin or other thick blister-padding tape

❑ First-aid tape and/or duct tape

❑ Ace bandages

❑ Gauze and nonstick dressings

❑ Antibacterial ointment

- A few over-the-counter medications like ibuprofen, acetaminophen, aspirin, and stomach antacids

  A more complete kit will include:

- Trauma shears

- Hand sanitizer

- "Sam" splint

- Tweezers

- Spare sunglasses

- Backup sunblock and/or lip balm

Repair Kit

While your first-aid kit is your "human repair kit," you may also want to carry equipment repair supplies in a repair kit. The longer and more committing the route, the more important repair readiness is. Without bringing the entire tool box, include items like:

A basic kit for most foreseeable equipment problems.

- ❏ Pliers or a Leatherman or similar multi-tool and/or pocketknife
- ❏ Small selection of screws like those used in most ski bindings
- ❏ Ski pole repair kit
- ❏ Hose clamps for repairing skis and/or poles
- ❏ Section of steel wire and/or cable or duct tape
- ❏ Steel wool in film canister, for stripped out screw holes
- ❏ Parachute cord
- ❏ 3 or 4 feet of duct tape in a small roll
- ❏ Spare buckles, batteries, and basket for ski poles and spare binding parts
- ❏ A variety of zip ties
- ❏ Epoxy
- ❏ Lighter (not shown)
- ❏ Extra ski wax and kicker skis that match the ski width for your tour
- ❏ Ski strap and a spare headlamp (for Murphy's Law repairs after dark)

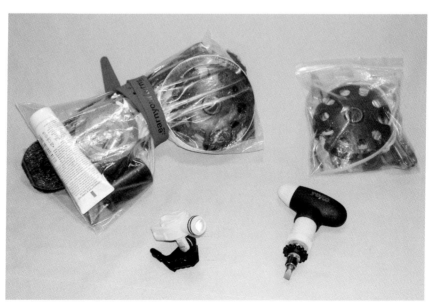

Kits of different sizes, with two essential tools: a clip-on headlamp (spare batteries are in the kit) and a ratchet screw driver.

I broke this binding on mile 1 of a 29-mile tour along the Teton Crest. I inserted a bent wire to hold the binding in place on its track. A simple repair is often all that's needed to save the day, but having tools and resources is critical.

As with the first-aid kit, if your repair kit is too large, ultimately it will slow you down or you'll feel like it's too big to bring and leave it at home. Carry the right tool or materials for the gear most likely to fail, and if a situation arises, your companions will be calling you "MacGyver" after the resourceful TV detective who seemed to be able to rig ingenious solutions with minimal materials. Perhaps the smallest and lightest kit might be a pocketknife and roll of duct tape. You would be surprised by the great number of things you can repair with a kit this small. In contrast, if you have everything but a knife and some duct tape, that repair-bench-in-a-pack will surely feel like dead weight.

CHAPTER 10

The Places You Can Go

Cross-country skiing can take you across all kinds of country, to places accessible in no other way and through conditions that only skis can allow you to navigate. Skis have been used to chart unexplored regions and discover unknown parts of the world for centuries.

Cross-country skiing can also provide employment and even a career. For those who love skiing, working close to what you love brings fulfillment. Sharing the love of skiing with others can even provide a higher level of contentment than skiing itself.

Conditions

Cross-country skiing can be done anywhere there is snow and appropriate terrain. However, that still leaves the factor of the snow surface, also called the conditions. Snow conditions can range from snowcat-groomed trails to supportable or breakable crust; from shallow snow to deep, "bottomless" powder; from new, dry snow to old, wet, slushy snow. And this list only begins to scratch the surface of possible conditions that may affect the skiing on any given day.

What's the snow like? With today's Web-based weather forecasting, "now-casting," and reporting, you can get a fairly accurate idea before you go of what to expect for snow conditions at all but the most remote areas. The snow conditions may guide or dictate your decision about where to go and what route to take. For example, in a low-snow situation, a route on a north-facing slope might be more likely to have consistent snow cover. Or if it's bitter cold, a route in the sun could be better. Conditions may also affect your decision about what kind of skis to take, if you have more than one set.

An avalanche awareness class can give you the tools you need to avoid avalanche terrain (the deeper understanding of when and how you can safely navigate avalanche terrain and interpret avalanche forecast information is beyond the scope of this work). To learn more about avalanches look up www.americanavalancheassociation.org or seach "avalanche basics."

Spring Corn

Spring corn represents one of the most enjoyable ski experiences available. Although referred to in seasonal terms, corn can occur at any time of year with the right weather conditions or combination of weather factors.

Spring corn refers to a condition where there is a crust on top of the snow that is supportable, meaning that it supports a skier's weight; a breakable crust—a crust you can't trust—will likely fail under a skier's weight and allow the skier to sink through the crust and curse. A firm, thick crust on top of the snowpack allows for travel just about anywhere as long as the crust remains supportable, even on steeper terrain. Crust is most amazing for providing a three-dimensional surface for skate skiing. Wind- and sun-

Crust cruising around a meadow on a cold spring morning.

sculpted snow can form a natural terrain park in gullies and around boulders. Skimming over refrozen drifts on skis is as close as you can get to flying with your feet on the ground.

For a crust to develop, temperatures must be warm and then cold frequently enough to melt and then subsequently refreeze the snow on top of the snowpack. This type of crust, known as a melt-freeze crust, forms with multiple days of ample sunlight or above-freezing temperatures in combination with enough cold or clear-sky nights. Crusts vary in strength and durability; a thicker or firmer crust—having frozen harder—will last longer and be less prone to breaking. A crust that is not frozen very deeply won't last as long under the warming rays of the spring sun. Take care when planning a tour not to commit to a route that the conditions will not support. If you get to the midpoint of your tour but can no longer stay "on top," it may take twice as long or more to finish the route or get back to where you started.

With more warming and more sunlight as the day goes on, the crust will deteriorate further. For the classic skier, crust cruising will require

Long shadows, magical reflections of snow, and amazing crust cruising in May.

no-wax skis or klister, while for the skate skier, waxing for the warming conditions can ensure that good glide is available throughout the tour.

Groomed Trail Systems

One way to beat the odds and ski on a predictably good surface is to go to one of the 500 or so groomed cross-country ski areas in the United States. There you can find instruction, rentals, a shop, and/or a five-star lodge, but perhaps most important, you'll also find regularly reconditioned snow that is molded into a smooth and consistent surface by hydraulic machinery at the skilled hands of a snowcat driver.

There are groomed cross-country ski areas in thirty of the fifty states. Many areas start grooming as soon as there is enough snow (as little as 8 to 12 inches, depending on density and other factors) and groom until the snow melts completely on parts of the trail, making it impassable to skiers and snowcats alike.

Groomed cross-country areas offer predictably good skiing conditions.

Grooming equipment as basic as a tracksetter pulled by a snowmobile can range from simple (under $400) to sophisticated ($4,500 or more).

Diesel-hydraulic snowcat groomers have two sets of tracks (treads) held together by metal "growsers," which run around wheels and provide traction to the tracks. The tracks, the blade on the front, and the tiller on the back are all powered by hydraulic transmission lines and a diesel engine. While the cost of buying and maintaining a snowcat is high, these machines do produce the highest quality grooming.

Check on current conditions at ski resorts and groomed areas by calling the area's "snow phone" line or by checking online.

Ungroomed Trailheads

Countless opportunities for cross-country skiing exist where there is publicly accessible land and enough snow cover. Options include trails or closed roads on USDA Forest Service lands, national parks, state parks, local pathways, city parks, and even on the fairways and paths on golf courses. Private lands may be an option as well, with advance permission or prior arrangement by a local pathways entity.

Where to Go

Plan a route that meets your objectives: Distance, exploration, and destinations such as lakes or waterfalls are all worth considering. Make sure that the route is within the fitness abilities of all your group members. If your tour becomes "epic" for some of your skiing friends, it may be more than memorable; so go where everyone has fun, and they'll want to ski again.

Cross-country skiing is not limited to groomed trails or short jaunts from a snowy trailhead. In fact, some of the most rewarding outings are the ones where you get farther away and cover significant terrain. Overnight trips to huts or to a snow-camping destination make for very special memories indeed. Here are a few considerations to help you prepare for such extended tours.

Know Your Route

Using a guidebook, topographical maps, or online resources such as Google Maps or Google Earth, plan your route to allow adequate time to cover the distance within daylight hours. Estimate your speed based on your average travel time, taking into account elevation gain, downhills (which can sometimes be slower than going up), and breaking trail. Establish a nonnegotiable "turnaround time" to trigger a retreat in the event of slow progress, so that you don't end up skiing out in the dark. Keep track of your route along the way and know where you are at all times, referencing landmarks to prevent getting lost. A GPS unit and/or a compass and map and knowledge of how to use them can help keep you on track.

Early Starts

Once you're late, you can't buy more time, so starting early is a great way to increase the amount of time between starting out and darkness. Other reasons to get an early start include time to relax and explore, skiing at a leisurely pace, and buffer time for wrong turns, equipment problems, injuries, or rescue. Changing conditions such as warming temperatures can slow your progress. You can always turn back before you get mired in sloppy snow or if the crust you're skiing on becomes breakable, but if starting an hour earlier would have allowed you to finish your route, wouldn't that have been so much better?

Fun for the Whole Family

This chapter celebrates the inclusiveness of cross-country skiing, welcoming skiers of all ages and abilities, all colors, countries, and creeds.

Kids

Cross-country skiing isn't just *open* to kids, it's an ideal way for kids to have fun and to develop social skills, fitness and coordination, and an appreciation of winter sports and winter itself. Many of the skills that adults work to learn come naturally to kids as they develop body awareness and the ability to move in the world. For example, younger children can learn to ski well through games, not just because they're having fun, but also because the skiing helps them achieve the game's goal. Further, they learn to ski "better" not by being taught, but by teaching themselves, instilling a love of learning.

Age-appropriate games, for a given skiing playgroup, can give kids another way to teach themselves new movements, while in pursuit of another goal. Team games for teens, or racing and chasing games for young skiers who have a competitive streak, and games of balance, coordination, and ball play all appeal to youngsters in different stages of development. Kids will find and make their own games with time and comfort on skis. Kids always seem to find a hill when there is one, and

Parks, fields, meadows, and other open spaces are great for exploring on cross-country skis.

they seem to love going up and down it. Playing on a hill is great for kids—once they've learned how to ski hills safely and well. When kids are good at stopping and turning, they're ready for jumping, racing, and other ski games on hills. Kids of all ages are learning about skiing etiquette and usually do well with a few rules about safety such as acknowledging clear right of way or stopping play when someone falls. For me as an educator, some of my most memorable moments on skis have been in the middle of a game with a bunch of kids, just having fun in the snow.

There is quite a bit to the art of teaching skiing to kids. In fact, PSIA has dedicated a separate three-level certification track to teaching kids called Children's Specialist. Just because there's a lot to know about teaching kids shouldn't be a reason for parents to shy away from getting out with their kids. Rather, parents should take every opportunity to go skiing with their children. It's important to make a conscious effort not to *teach* kids, instead focusing on having fun and giving them as many chances to *play* on skis as possible.

Keeping skiing family-friendly can be a challenge. A strategy that works for many skiing families is the use of sleds.

Pulks, Chariots, and Other Sleds

Pulk is the name for a cargo sled rigged with a hipbelt harness for hands-free skiing. The use of pulks for children may seem like a relatively recent adaptation, but children have been riding in sleds behind skiing parents for probably as long as there have been sleds and skis. Fancier pulk designs may include a padded floor, a backrest, and even a zippered cover to optimize passenger warmth.

Filling a void for today's active families, companies like Chariot have produced kid-carrying conveyances that can be rigged with skis for snow, with wheels for bike towing or jogging, and with swiveling rollers to make a more maneuverable stroller. Although more

Mom and Dad get to ski, while junior enjoys winter inside the cozy confines of a carrier.

expensive, these folding multisport rigs are very well designed, with everything from zip-off clear window panels for hot summer rides to shock absorbers. Additionally, these rigs can turn mom and dad's rolling or skiing exercise into a nap-friendly environment for a bouncing baby, making them a must-have for the active family.

Tracksetter Sleds

Setting track with a sled is not a new idea, but using a convertible sled is. A sled like this is pulled behind an adult. The weight of a child or snow in the sled leaves an impression of skiable tracks. If a child becomes tired while skiing, the parent can turn the sled around, putting the ski tips forward, and let the child climb in for a ride.

Your Own Nordic Snow Park

Where better for kids to play on skis than in your own backyard, or a nearby city park, golf course, or open field? In our small front yard, we have groomed multiple loops that climb and dip, cross walkways, and

A handy, light tracksetter sled is great for laying a track or giving a ride to a tired skier.

go in and out of our snow fort. Basically, with a little bit of work and a lot of fun, we built a playground for little skiers. The kids are entertained. Mom and dad get a workout. And hot cocoa is never far away.

Seniors

While learning to cross-country ski poses challenges and comes with inherent risks, the rewards can be great: exercise, health on a number of levels, and enjoyment of the winter environment. Many skiers who learn to cross-country ski before they reach the age where, for example, brittle bones are a concern can ski actively right on into old age. The oldest participant to complete the 2011 Birkebeiner 50 kilometer race in Wisconsin was 86 years old. I hope I'm skiing when I'm that old too.

Adaptive

Adaptive skiing encompasses a host of disabilities, or as one adaptive instructor/educator colleague likes to point out: "We're all just temporarily able-bodied." Adaptive skiing teaches skiers how to bypass limitations and adapt themselves or their equipment to make skiing accessible. Adaptive instructors study how to make skiing available to individuals with developmental delays, spinal cord injury, amputation, traumatic brain injury, Down syndrome, multiple sclerosis, critical illness, vision or hearing challenges, ADD/ADHD, autism, or Asperger's syndrome, among others.

Overcoming a disability is extremely rewarding for the individual, his or her family members, and the instructor. Conquering the seemingly impossible is the objective, and meeting the challenge inspires confidence and affirmation.

For more information about adaptive cross-country skiing, seek out an adaptive winter sports program near you. The Winter Paralympic Games are held every four years and the Winter Special Olympics take place annually. Both are inspirational gathering points for people with disabilities.

Everyone

Cross-country skiing can be enjoyed by everyone. The barriers to getting out on skis can all be overcome, save one: no snow. When snow is a long distance away, or good snow is unlikely, skiing can wait, but if you seek out snow, it almost always yields a pleasant surprise or two. And when snow is overwhelming to the general population, like the storm that dumped up to 5 feet of the white stuff and paralyzed New York City in 2011, you can be among those storm opportunists with a perfect solution. With a set of skis you can exercise, go to the store, ski down the street to your friend's house, and probably get all the way across town if you had to. If everyone had a pair of skis, we'd be ready for the next city snowstorm gridlock.

The fact is, if you can walk, you can ski, so think ahead to the next time you'll be on skis, on snow, reveling in winter and getting the most out of life. If your experience is at all like mine, you'll have moments so cool and so memorable that you too will wish you could share it with everyone.

Appendix A: Resources

No introduction to cross-country skiing would be complete without pointing the way to the wealth of resources that are out there to inform and guide the developing skier. Whether it's racing, recreational, light touring, or backcountry skiing; teaching or coaching; or getting your kids (or parents) going, there are books, magazines, and other resources that can enrich your knowledge and understanding of technique, equipment, waxing, training, and much more.

Here is a brief list of the best books, magazines, websites, and video resources to help fuel your passion for cross-country skiing:

Books

Cross-Country Skiing: Building Skills for Fun and Fitness, by Steve Hindman, 2005. Hindman, a twelve-year member of the PSIA Nordic Demonstration Team, brings together his accumulated knowledge about skiing and learning to ski. This compilation of all aspects of Nordic skiing is an in-depth reference for skiers of all levels.

Training Cross-Country Skiing, by Katrin Barth and Hubert Bruhl, 2006. Translated from German, this book has detailed illustrations and would be a great gift for the budding cross-country youth competitor.

Nordic Technical Manual, published by PSIA, authored by PSIA Nordic Demonstration Team members, 2005. This handbook of teaching and technique for cross-country and telemark instructors goes in-depth on skiing models and skills and introduces the Stepping Stones model, a teaching method for matching a tailored progression to the needs, desires, and abilities of a given student.

Magazines

Ski Trax, "North America's Nordic Ski Magazine," publishes four issues a year with cross-country racing as its primary focus. Backcountry, destination areas, and equipment topics are also covered and there are great columns on technique, training, diet, US Ski Team vignettes, and much more. See www.skitrax.com.

Cross Country Skier, a US-based publication, covers equipment, technique, and XC ski reports and claims to be the oldest journal on recreational Nordic skiing in the world. See www.crosscountryskier.com.

Master Skier, a newsprint-turned-color-glossy-journal magazine is aimed at serious Nordic racers of thirty-plus years. Racers' stories and news of innovations in training, technique, and equipment are included. See www.masterskier.com.

Websites

Cross Country Ski Areas Association is the nonprofit organization for a network of 270-plus member areas. This extensive site has detailed videos, podcasts, and articles on how to get started, where to ski, plus links to resorts and grooming reports for the public and pages for suppliers, member areas, and the press. See www.xcski.org.

Cross Country Ski World features headlines from magazine and news websites like those listed above. Claiming to be "designed for absolute beginners thru die-hard athletes," it has more links than original material for news, educational articles, and information devoted to XC skiing and racing. It's also the home of American Cross Country Skiers (AXCS), a master's racing organization. See www.xcskiworld.com.

The Faster Skier is a rich source for the die-hard racer or follower of junior, masters, and World Cup competition, with timely race news and authoritative technique articles. See www.fasterskier.com.

Cross-Country Skiing Online is an exhaustive ad-supported, information-rich reference site for all things cross-country related. See www.cross-countryski.com.

DVDs

On-Snow Technique Drills: Training with a Purpose, 2011, CXC's new on-snow technique drills DVD for skiers of all levels with Jason Cork

Cross-Country Skiing Dryland Drills and Fundamentals, 2010, with Andrew Newell and Liz Stephen

Advanced Nordic Skiing, 2009, with a detailed technical analysis is
provided by former Olympic athletes, World Cup gold medalists, and
coaches synthesized into professional narrative script. By Canada's
XCZONE.TV

Cross-Country Technique Progressions, 2009, with Yuriy Gusev, Bryan
Fish, Matt Whitcomb, and Garrott Kuzzy

Nordic Ski Training Secrets for High Performance Sport, 2007, starring
Ed McNee, Dr. Penny Werthner, and Ole Einar Bjoerndalen

Cross-Country Skiing, 2006, with Butch Delong and Taylor Overbey

Learn to Nordic Ski, 2006, with Lise Meloche, Lynn Bermel, and David
McMahon

Nordic Skiing Technique, 2006, with Lise Meloche, Gudrun Pfleuger, Phil
Villeneuve, and David McMahon

Unlimited Nordic Skiing, 2003, with David McMahon, Lise Meloche, and
Beckie Scott

YouTube

YouTube offers numerous videos on cross-country ski instruction,
training techniques, waxing tips, and other information related to the
sport. To find these clips, go to www.YouTube.com and put the channel
name listed here into the search field. Some channels only have a few
videos, while others are loaded with content.

BryanFishski: 2- to 3-minute videos of top racers training or racing with
music and/or narration by US Ski Team coach Bryan Fish

Ssrknordic: short clips of top-ranked skiers performing various
techniques

Nordicskisource: waxing tips and cross-country videos and event
reporting

k2nicol: Keith Nicol is a member of the Canadian Association of Nordic
Ski Instructors (CANSI) and a cross-country ski technique columnist
for *Ski Trax* magazine.

Many of the Nordic ski wax companies (Swix, Toko, Holmenkol, Start,
Rex, SkiFast, Rode, Vauhti, and others) have great videos available
online for the searching.

Appendix B: What to Bring

In addition to your first-aid kit and repair kit, you'll need some key items—something like the ten essentials—for winter travel:

- **Skis, boots, poles**—skis, waxed for the conditions; boots, warm and dry at the start of the day; and poles, with straps adjusted to your hands and gloves.

- **Hat, gloves, buff**—to borrow some wisdom from another proverb: "Two hats are better than one." One heavyweight hat is great if it's cold and you're not very active, but even at temperatures well below freezing, skiing generates enough heat that a heavy hat is too much. Instead, bring two lightweight hats. If you need to adjust for conditions, layering up or down is as easy as doffing or donning the chapeau stored in your pocket. Mittens are surely the warmest in handwear, but lack often-needed dexterity with bindings and poles. Two pairs of gloves ensure quick relief if one pair gets wet and fingers cold. Better yet may be a layered glove system, with a leather-palmed, lighter-weight breathable glove and a shell glove or mitten to go over it. The "buff" is a neck gaiter made of Lycra.

- **Shell layer**—you may need to be prepared for wind and blowing snow, wet snow, or outright rain. If conditions are warm, fair, and stable, bringing a layer as light as a windshirt might be enough to fill the shell niche on a shorter tour.

- **Puffy layer**—the shell layer is great for the elements of wind and precipitation, but nothing keeps the heat in like good insulation around the body's core. This is the layer you can pull out to keep your muscles and core warm when you stop for food and water, navigation, or rest. The puffy layer and the shell together can keep you even toastier.

- **Skin protection, sun protection, eye protection**—this might include sunblock, chapstick, a billed cap or brimmed hat, and sunglasses and/or goggles.

- **Food, water, chocolate**—snacks are an obvious addition for on-the-go energy, but what makes a good snack? Something that tastes good, is easy-to-eat and nutritive, and has a balance of carbs, fats, and protein. Many energy bars miss the first point, being tasty. Choice menu items, like smoked gouda, might not be so easy to eat, but that doesn't mean you shouldn't bring them at all.

- **Map, compass, phone**—see the discussion in chapter 9 about navigation and emergency preparedness.

What to Bring Checklists

Day Tours

- ❏ Hat
- ❏ Gloves
- ❏ Sunglasses and/or goggles
- ❏ Map and compass/GPS
- ❏ Lighter
- ❏ Small repair kit
- ❏ First-aid kit
- ❏ Food and water

Overnight Trips

- ❏ All of the above and . . .
- ❏ Shovel
- ❏ Sleeping bag and pad
- ❏ Tent and/or tarp
- ❏ Stove and fuel
- ❏ Booties
- ❏ Neck gaitor/buff
- ❏ "Puffy" down or poly coat
- ❏ Extra socks
- ❏ Extra hat and mittens

Glossary

alignment: The position of body parts relative to one another that minimizes muscular effort needed to maintain body position (stance)

alpine skiing: The sport of skiing that evolved from Nordic skiing with the invention of ski lifts and locked-heel bindings

backcountry skiing: Any kind of skiing done away from developed land, open roads, or lift-assisted ski resorts, on cross-country, randonee (alpine touring), or telemark skis, in which avalanche awareness and self-rescue capabilities are important safety skills

balancing movements: Tensioning of muscles or movements of the core, legs, or arms to maintain or recover balance

bounding: A dry-land training exercise for classic cross-country skiing in which the athlete springs ahead off one leg and then lands and balances on the opposite foot

camber: The bend in an unweighted ski. In classic skis, which have a "double camber," this bend keeps the middle of the ski, called the wax pocket, off the snow when partially weighted, and lets the skier press the wax pocket into the snow when fully weighted. On skate skis, which have a single camber, full body weight leads to even weight distribution along the ski for optimum glide.

classic skiing: The traditional form of cross-country skiing that utilizes skis waxed for grip or with waxless, patterned bases. The term is commonly used to distinguish diagonal stride–based racing technique from freestyle (skating) technique.

core: The collection of specific muscles in the body's torso, including the abdominal, oblique, gluteal, and back muscles, that stabilize the body, and are utilized to provide optimum efficiency in skiing

diagonal skate: The form of skate skiing most like walking. The skier maintains a wide "V" position of the skis, and the pole plants are timed with the transfer of weight onto the opposite ski.

double pole: A classic cross-country maneuver in which the arms and torso are the sole source of propulsion. Both arms are simultaneously brought forward to begin poling, with a distinct whole-body forward lean and abdominal crunch of the upper body over the poles.

double pole kick: A classic skiing technique to carry speed up a slight hill using a double pole with a wax set for push-off during arm extension, and forward leg swing during double pole compression

dynamic balance: Balance in motion; when the center of mass moves inside and outside the base of support, for example, in double poling, the skier's forward lean might cause her to fall forward, but for the "catch" of the poles, translating into forward motion. Dynamic balance is critical in all forms of skiing.

falling forward: The body position used for classic and skate skiing; a whole-body, forward-leaning position that results in more efficient technique

foot pass: When the feet pass each other in each stride in classic skiing, seen when looking at the skier from the side. The body position should be aligned and "stacked" at the moment when the feet pass each other.

glide wax: Paraffin-like hydrocarbon or fluorocarbon substance rubbed, wiped, or ironed on skis, to decrease friction and suction between ski bases and snow

grip wax: Wax for classic skiing that allows the ski both to grip the snow when pressured and to glide over the snow when not weighted. Depending on snow conditions, the appropriate grip wax might be harder for colder temperatures, or softer and sticky for warm or wet temperatures.

herringbone: A technique for climbing hills in which the skier faces uphill with ski tips separated into a "V" and walks up the hill, alternating feet, on the skis' inside edges to avoid slipping backward

interval: A duration of higher intensity exercise, often in the 3- to 6-minute range, designed to promote development of speed and power

klister: Soft, sticky, liquid wax (usually in a tube) applied to a shorter kick zone for grip on wet or refrozen snow

lactate threshold: During anaerobic workouts such as sprints, a muscle condition in which the pumping of the blood is no longer sufficient to remove the lactate produced by the contraction of the muscles

light touring: Cross-country skiing that does not utilize prepared tracks. Equipment is generally heavier than for classic skiing or skating, and walking, striding, skating, and downhill techniques may all be used.

marathon skate: Maneuver that combines double poling with one ski in the track, while skating with the other ski out of the track

no-pole skate: V0; skating without using poles for propulsion, when speeds are too great for poling to generate more momentum

Nordic skiing: The oldest form of skiing, characterized by use of a free-heel binding; includes Nordic downhill, cross-country skiing, and backcountry touring

overspeed: A workout in which you ski faster than you can maintain, in order to develop more fast-twitch muscle capability, and therefore speed

progression: Activities and movements in a sequence that starts simple and increases in complexity, resulting in a "finished form" such as diagonal stride or V2

proprioception: "Sensing near"; awareness of body parts and their location in space and in relation to one another

ptex: Polyethylene ski base material

sidecut: The hourglass shape of a ski; a ski is typically wider at the tip and tail and narrower at the waist; many skate ski models have "negative sidecut" where the tip is narrower than the waist.

skate turn: A turning technique, also used to generate propulsion, where the skier makes a turn by using a series of skating steps

skating: A method of propulsion in which the skier pushes from foot to foot while maintaining the skis in a diverging "V" position. The inside edges of the skis are alternately engaged and the skier uses a strong push-off from ski to ski to move forward. Also known as freestyle

sprint: A shorter race of 1 to 5 kilometers; a high-intensity training interval; to ski as fast as possible

step turn: While gliding, using a series of steps to make a turn

structure: A pattern of small grooves in a ski's base that is used to break up suction from the snow

tactics: Choosing where to go and when to apply different techniques

Telemark: The region in Norway where the telemark turn originated

telemark turn: A turn accomplished by sliding the feet apart fore and aft to increase fore-aft stability, lifting the heel on the back ski and edging both skis to turn. The right ski leads for a left turn and the left ski leads for a right turn.

tempo: Rate of repetition for body movements like striding, skating, and poling

transition: Gradual or abrupt shift from one technique to another, often to accommodate changing terrain or snow conditions

wax pocket: The area in the middle of double-cambered classic skis that is patterned or waxed for grip. Classic skiers engage the wax or the base pattern for traction by de-cambering the ski with weight and push-off force.

wax set: In classic skiing, the ability of the skier to de-camber the ski so the wax pocket grips the snow, providing traction

wedge: A useful way of managing speed and/or stopping on skis, in which the skis are in an "A" position (tips together) and both skis are on their inside edge

wedge christie: A turn in which the skier steers the skis into a wedge relationship at the turn initiation, then in the control phase or later in the turn, the skier steers the skis into a parallel (christie) relationship.

weight transfer: Movement of weight and balance from one foot to the other

Index

About the Author

Scotty McGee is the current PSIA Nordic Team coach and senior manager for Guides, Nordic, Adaptive, and Race at Jackson Hole Mountain Sports School. He's been deeply involved in skiing and outdoor education since his college days, when he first instructed cross-country skiing and  supervised the telemark programs for the legendary Dartmouth Outing Club. He has taught skiing, trained instructors, and guided in the Tetons and other ranges for resorts, colleges, private outfitters, and nonprofits.

McGee is among the most widely certified members of the PSIA Nordic Team, with certifications in ski instruction, avalanche safety, and guiding. He is Certified Level III in Nordic Track, Nordic Downhill, and Backcountry. Scott is a regular contributor to *The Professional Skier* and for the last five years has written a regular Tele Technique column featuring photomontages for *Ski Trax*. He's also been widely published in other ski instruction publications.

Not just an academic, McGee thrives on competition too, and has numerous top finishes in local tele competitions and a top-fifteen finish in an FIS Telemark World Cup GS.

A past president and racer for the US Telemark Ski Association, McGee enjoys applying his skills to racing, all-mountain skiing, and backcountry travel.

McGee's latest passion is backcountry skate skiing, and to date he has posted over twenty trans-Teton tours on light gear and has completed other distance tours in other ranges. An all-season mountaineer, McGee has been guiding for Exum Mountain Guides and relishes his summer training regimen of leading climbs and peak ascents in the Tetons.